RUSSIAN ORGANIZED CRIME IN BRANSON, MISSOURI

Russian Organized Crime in Branson, Missouri

The Seven Year Chase, Arrest and Conviction of Serguei

Jesse E Stoker

Columbus, Ohio

I have tried my best to recreate events, locations and conversations from my memories of them and copies of documents and news articles available to me from open sources. In order to protect people's privacy, in some instances I have changed the names of individuals and places, some identifying characteristics and details such as physical features, occupations and places of residence and/or business.

Some names and identifying details have been changed to protect the individuals' privacy.

The views and opinions expressed in this book are solely those of the author and do not reflect the views or opinions of Gatekeeper Press. Gatekeeper Press is not to be held responsible for and expressly disclaims responsibility of the content herein.

Russian Organized Crime In Branson, Missouri: The Seven Year Chase, Arrest and Conviction of Serguei

Published by Gatekeeper Press
2167 Stringtown Rd, Suite 109
Columbus, OH 43123-2989
www.GatekeeperPress.com

Copyright © 2022 by Jesse E Stoker

All rights reserved. Neither this book, nor any parts within it may be sold or reproduced in any form or by any electronic or mechanical means, including information storage and retrieval systems, without permission in writing from the author. The only exception is by a reviewer, who may quote short excerpts in a review.

The editorial work for this book is entirely the product of the author. Gatekeeper Press did not participate in and is not responsible for any aspect of this element.

Library of Congress Control Number: 2022936890

ISBN (paperback): 9781662926525

Contents

Acknowledgments

Introduction

Chapter One
    Immigration and Naturalization Service and Me   1

Chapter Two
    The First Investigation 1999-2001   15

Chapter Three
    The In-Between Case Period 2001-2004   39

Chapter Four
    Investigation Two – A New Beginning   63

Chapter Five
    Midwest Hotel Management Corporation (MWHMC)   79

Chapter Six
    Deep Dive to Arrests   99

Chapter Seven
    Evidence and Charges   131

Chapter Eight
    Witness Intimidation   151

Chapter Nine
    Pleas, Sentencings, and Serguei Still Not Giving Up   183

Chapter Ten
    Epilogue   195

SOURCES

Book Dedication

I would like to dedicate this book to my family. My wife Janet, the love of my life; my children, Chad, Mike, and Janelle, their spouses, and our grandchildren, who through the years dealt with absences at birthday parties, holidays, picnics, sports events, and concerts. They had to deal with long days and nights, call outs at all times, never knowing when I would have to go or get home, all so I could fulfill my dreams of being in law enforcement, a criminal investigator. If it wasn't for my family, their love for me, and their continued prayers, I would never have accepted Christ as my Lord and Savior in October 1992. Because of Him, and the sacrifice that He made on the cross for the world and His grace and mercy, I have been saved and have eternal life in heaven with Him.

I love you all from the bottom of my heart and owe you all so very much that I will never be able to repay.

Acknowledgments

Writing a book for the first time, is not as easy as I thought it would be. But, thanks to the patience and assistance of my wife who assisted me with the formatting and editing of this book and its contents. Because of that patience and assistance, I was able to accomplish this task.

I would also like to thank Gatekeeper Press for the hard work, diligence, and professionalism in continued communication throughout the process after I finally made the decision to have it published, in providing me with the book I was looking for to tell the story that I believe needed to be told.

Lastly, I would like to thank my granddaughter Abby Fults. Who with a Bachelor of Fine Arts in Graphic Design from Park University in Parkville, Missouri was able to design for me a book cover that I believe would draw the attention of persons who are familiar with Branson Missouri and the surrounding area in hopes they would have a desire to read this story.

Thank you all so very much. Without your assistance and patience, this book could not have been completed.

Introduction

"Stop!" "Stop typing!" "Stop what you are doing!" "Get away from the computer!" I ran up to the back of Serguei and grabbed him by the back of the collar of his shirt and blue jean jacket and pulled him with a substantial amount of force out of his chair and away from the computer just as a loud noise came from the computer that sounded like an explosion. Serguei yelled in Russians something I'm sure was not very nice, and since I don't speak Russian, I can only imagine what he said. Serguei was thrown face first onto the floor and my gun was put at the back of his neck. Just as John Cress my co-case agent and partner in the investigation and I both got on top of him and I told him "Serguei, be quiet it's Stoker with Immigration!" Then he calmed down as I handcuffed him, John and I then lifted him off of the floor and took him upstairs to the dining room table where it was our intent to interview him while the other agents and officers completed the search of his residence.

This was the arrest of Serguei D. Choukline (Serguei), a citizen of Russia and a Lawful Permanent Resident in the United States.

This book is not just about our investigation of Serguei Choukline, but also about Russian Organized Crime in the United States. How a person with an organized crime background may treat their employees if they're involved in this type of fraud. These are things that an employer who uses a Russian employment service may look for in the treatment of the employees they use. This book identifies Russian Organized Crime in southern Missouri, or at least Serguei Demitrievsky Choukline wanted his employees to believe that he was a member of organized crime. He played on that claim to control his employees.

Russian Organized Crime is like that of organized crime groups of the past in America like the Genovese, Gotti, Al Capone, Lucky Luciano, or any other mob figures. The only difference is, depending on the group could be a lot more violent. In this instance, with Serguei, there was only a threat of violence most of the time except for one incident where Serguei beat an employee in the presence of the other employees stating "If you screw with me, this is what will happen to you. I have friends with INS and with the police and will have you arrested and sent back to your country!"

Serguei's organization or claim to such, is much like the Drug Cartels, in that Serguei threatened his employees with violence, kept their passports in many instances, controlled their movements to and from work, where they slept and directed who they shared a room with whether the people sharing a room knew each other or not and it didn't matter if they were young or old or male or female. The threats, the beat downs, keeping documents, controlling work and housing, falls right in line with slave labor and involuntary servitude.

Serguei could put off a flare of being a nice guy. If I had just met him at a meeting or something I could see how he was seen as a likeable guy. He has an appearance of cooperation and working with other groups like the police, better business bureau, hotel, and motel industries to provide workers, but to his employees, he is a very manipulative and demanding businessman and employer.

Serguei had a wife and son, and his wife at least engaged in his business adventure of supplying employees to the hospitality industry in and around Branson and Springfield, Missouri, supplying foreign nationals to fill the vacant positions that the businesses claim that they cannot fill with the local employee pools. Serguei's wife became involved in the criminal activity and was determined to be just as involved as Serguei. Serguei did all of the heavy lifting, but his wife was the bookkeeper of the business.

This book details the investigation from the records that I have been able to maintain through the years since I have retired. It speaks to Serguei's travels abroad to work with travel agencies to recruit foreign nationals from the foreign labor pool for his businesses. His travels resulted in the filing of eighteen fraudulent applications with INS/HSI, the United States Department of Labor, and the Missouri Department of Labor for more than three hundred foreign nationals to fill vacant employee positions in the Branson and Springfield, Missouri area in the United States.

You will see how Serguei didn't care about being a citizen of the United States by his own words, all he cared about was the American dollar, American money. He wasn't trying to be a credit to the United States citizenry, he just wanted to take advantage of not only the employees he had working for him, but the American businesses he served.

This is just a brief overview of what you will read about. What most people do not realize is that this type of activity goes on all over the United States and if this is done in the small communities of Branson and Springfield, Missouri, imagine what is happening in the big city. The big city like New York, Los Angeles, Miami, places where many people do not care where they get their employees from as long as they can meet the needs of the customer. The customer does not care most of the time because they want what they want when they want it and there is no matter where or from whom it came.

However, you will see in this book how many of the foreign workers began to turn on Serguei, because they saw how in the United States of America there are freedoms that allow them to come to the officials without fear of repercussion for their complaints and allegations. You will see the diligence of law enforcement agencies who over a total period of 7 years, worked tirelessly to get these employees out and away from their fear of Serguei and his threats.

Serguei and his co-conspirators were arrested and charged with several allegations of fraud, false statement, and other crimes.

An involved criminal investigation of this sort with multiple facets is not done overnight like you see on television. There has to be determination of a crime, evidence, collection of evidence, presentation to the United States Attorney, grand jury subpoenas, search warrants, arrests, charges, trial subpoenas, interviews of witnesses and the trial itself. Depending on the magnitude of the investigation and evidence, the investigation can go on for a period of time.

In this investigation you will see the two very different career paths of two totally different individuals. One on a criminal path of greed, recognition, and importance for himself, and the other on a path toward truth and justice. In this instance, the first investigation was three years long, and the second was four years long. This is not television, this is reality.

Chapter One

Immigration and Naturalization Service and Me

The Immigration and Naturalization Service, or INS, has been around almost since the beginning of the country. Of course, it was not known as the INS until it was created in 1933, but before that the control of our borders, deportations, and exclusions from the United States and who was and was not allowed to enter or come into the United States was under congress to make the laws, but the individual states had the authority to enforce the laws. It was not until after the first Federal Service Center at Ellis Island, New York was constructed in 1891, Immigration violations came under federal jurisdiction and only federal authorities could deport. However, the actual enforcement didn't begin until sometime in 1892.

The United States was created by the completion of the Declaration of Independence in 1776. For those of you who do not know your History, the Declaration of Independence was signed on July 4, 1776, and therefore we celebrate Independence Day on July the 4th each year, to celebrate our independence for Great Britain.

The first law that was put into place allowing for the deportation of aliens from the United States was granted to the President of the United States in 1778, just two years after the creation of this country. This law identified as "The Alien Sedition Act," allowed the President of the United States to deport any foreign national determined to be dangerous to the United States and it also imposed a 14-year residency requirement to anyone that wanted to become a United States citizen. That requirement when I retired was three years if the foreign national is married to a United States citizen and five years for a person for instance that was married to a Lawful Permanent Resident.

The first laws that were put on the books to control the foreign labor in the United States was created in 1795. Many laws were put into place dealing with the control of the entry into the United States from its creation until now. These laws ranged from how long a person could remain in the United States, under what conditions a person could be denied entry to the reasons a person can be deported.

The controls of this authority fell under many different departments within the United States government.

- 1864- The first centralized control of Immigration was enacted under the Department of State.
- 1891-The Immigration Act of 1891 created the Bureau of Immigration, which fell within the jurisdiction of the United States Treasury Department. Prior to this date, the laws were established by the federal government,

but as I previously said, were enforced by the individual states until 1892.

- 1924 - The United States Border Patrol was created under the United States Department of Labor.

- 1933 - Still the Bureau of Immigration under the Treasury Department, has now become the Immigration and Naturalization Service, and in

- 1940 - The Immigration and Naturalization Service was placed under the authority of the United States Attorney and the Department of Justice. And it remained there until

- 2003 - When it was joined with several other agencies to create the new Department of Homeland Security, Immigration and Customs Enforcement, with several sub agencies such as Homeland Security Investigations where I worked.

Investigations throughout the time of this agency involved many different criminal investigations that I am sure many of you did not even realize the agency enforced. We conducted fraud investigations, not just any fraud but fraud that involved marriage fraud, visa fraud, identity theft, citizenship fraud, Naturalization Fraud, false statements on applications and to agents (just like the FBI). We also conducted investigations involving, guns, gangs, drugs, terrorism, and many other offenses against the United States. Under INS, there also had to be a nexus to foreign nationals. Any offense that involved a person from a foreign country that is illegally present or is a permanent resident in the United States fell under our jurisdiction to investigate.

United States citizens could be investigated and charged if they were involved in the smuggling of illegal aliens into the United States or if they obtained their own citizenship by fraud. Now that we have merged with agencies such as the United States Customs Service to form the Department of Homeland Security, this is no longer a requirement.

The INS identified who could or could not enter the United States. For instance, those who had diseases, those who were destitute and could not provide for themselves and depended on the federal or state governments for handouts. It was not until the early forties when foreign nationals were allowed to claim political asylum to enter the United States. Nothing like what it is today, when the borders are open, anyone can apply for asylum for just about any reason. In the past, if a person crossed another country to enter the United States they had to stay or remain in that country to file their applications and wait until their application was approved. Donald Trump brought that back into play, but Joe Biden has tried to return to the previous way of allowing everyone to come into this great country.

I had never even thought of being a part of the INS, as a career. I was working with the Department of Defense as a police officer on a military base near Kansas City, Missouri. This position was considered at the time more of a Security Guard position rather than a law enforcement position. I wanted to be in law enforcement, which was my desire for a career. A co-worker had applied for a detention officers' position with the INS. At that time, the INS like most federal law enforcement agencies had an age limit of 35 years of age to start and had to be retired at the latest age of 55 years of age, giving them 20 years in what was known as a law enforcement or covered position. My co-worker had just retired from the military at 38 years of age and exceeded the age of acceptance for the position, and there were no exemptions for those serving in the military other than points for prior service. He applied for the position and was denied the position due to his age. He returned to work a couple of days later and told me I needed to put in for the position as I was only 28 in 1984. So, I did, I applied for the job.

I was already a federal or government employee with the Department of Defense, and had been since December 1982, but was trying to start a new career in federal law enforcement. I put on my best slacks and sport jacket, tie and my military patent leather shoes that kept their shine. Trying to make the best impression or presentation that I could for my interview. I sat in an interview for about two hours with the District Director (DD), Deputy District Director (DDD), and the Supervisory Detention and Deportation Officer (SDDO). I was asked all kinds of questions relating to family, military career, background in law enforcement, as I was previously a Reserve Police Officer in a small suburb of Kansas City metropolitan area, and a Reserve Deputy Sheriff with the Wyandotte County Sheriff Department in Kansas City, Kansas. I had worked road patrol, jail, and warrants. I knew about transporting and caring for prisoners in my custody. As you can see, I really wanted to be in law enforcement. After the interview, I was sent out to the outer office of the secretary to wait. In about 10 minutes, the SDDO came out and gave me a preliminary offer for the position of an Immigration Detention Officer which was then known as an IDO, in the Kansas City Office. I am guessing that Serguei was probably in the Military about this time deciding his own career path.

Now, I had a collateral career going at the same time, as I was in the Air Force Reserves. I was active-duty Air Force during the end of the Vietnam War from 1974 to 1975, At the end of the war, they were beginning to downsize the military and I had the opportunity to go into the Air Force Reserves which I did. I was subsequently in the Reserve Security Police and then retired as a Special Agent with the Air Force Office of Special Investigations (AFOSI) where I spent my last five years. No, there is no such person or there was not at that time, a bionic or six-million-dollar man. I subsequently retired in 1999 after 25 years of good service with an Honorable Discharge.

I was a Detention Officer from 1984 until 1987 and was promoted to the position of a Special Agent in 1987. From 1987 until 1990, I was assigned to the Alien Criminal Apprehension Program or ACAP. In this program I traveled to all the Federal, State, and local jails and prisons in the State of Kansas, and the western half of the State of Missouri. This was our area of responsibility as it came to conducting interviews of foreign nationals in custody. Our duty was to determine if the foreign nationals that we interviewed were deportable from the United States based on their convictions. If they were, I would place a detainer on them with the institution and they would be turned over to INS upon their release from jail. I was also responsible for identifying and locating those that were released prior to being found by INS while still in jail, obtaining their conviction records to determine if they were deportable. If they were, then myself and my partner, Rick, would locate them, arrest them, and place them in removal proceedings.

There were a couple of interviews I specifically remember from those days, one being the interview of a citizen of Mexico who had been involved in the killing of a Mexican Federal Police Officer, and when he crossed into the United States he shot and seriously injured one of our own Border Patrol Agents. When I conducted interviews, I would attempt to get their immigration file from the records center to review before I did the interview. As I reviewed his immigration file, I remembered hearing his name while I was at the academy in Georgia. This person crossed the border illegally with a friend and both were observed transporting what appeared to be a large quantity of narcotics by two of our Border Patrol Agents who then commenced to track them from where they crossed. As they tracked them, they were able to determine that they had split up so one agent followed one and the other agent followed the second alien.

As the Border Patrol Agent following the second alien the person I am going to interview, rounded an Arroyo and observed this guy sitting in an old lawn chair holding a semi-automatic rifle who then opened fire on the Border Patrol Agent. The agent was shot through the ankle on one foot shot, in another place I don't remember where that was, and shot in the testicles as he laid on the ground, all the time returning fire with his shotgun, wounding the alien. His partner heard the gunfire and returned to the location of the second Border Patrol Agent. The alien was taken into custody. The first Border Patrol Agent was calling for assistance but because they were in a low area, the radios could not hit the radio repeater, no one could hear them. They could hear other agents talking but could not get out. The first Border Patrol Agent had to dress the wounds as best he could and then go to a higher location to use the radio to get out. What I can remember from being told the story in the academy, it took about two hours for assistance to arrive and get the injured Border Patrol Agent to a hospital. The outcome of the agent is that he survived the attack of this criminal, teaches occasionally at the academy, and actually participates regularly in running with various Border Patrol classes.

As far as the alien, I went to Leavenworth Federal Prison to interview him, of course determined that he was illegally present in the United States and was deportable and he was placed in removal proceedings. Since he was identified as a flight risk due to a previous escape attempt while in custody in a jail in Pecos, Texas, we made arrangements to house him at Leavenworth Federal Prison until his deportation court date with INS. We went to the prison and escorted him to the INS Office with several vehicles, with heavily armed agents inside. Of course, he was ordered deported from the United States to Mexico. We then escorted him back to the prison to be housed until an Immigration airplane could be arranged to pick him up and take him to the border. A couple of weeks later, we went through the same process and this time took him from prison to the Immigration flight at KCI Airport, where he was flown to the United States Mexican Border and was turned over to the Mexican authorities.

We found out that the night before our escort from Leavenworth to the INS Office for his hearing, our District Director was meeting some other Immigration Officers that he knew and were visiting Kansas City at a happy hour and was talking in public about our escort. From what I hear, he was saying nothing would happen, and this was good practice for the agents in a place for everyone and his brother to hear.

Well, it turned out that the illegal alien that shot the Border Patrol Agent was convicted in Mexico and was sent to prison. There, he paid a guard at the prison $1,500.00 to smuggle him a mini submachine gun of some sort and he and ten others attempted a prison break. In the process of the prison break, he shot and killed a prison guard and was in turn himself shot and killed by another guard. There was a news article from Mexico about the attempted Prison Break that made its way to the desk of the District Director, and it was never spoken of again. I don't know for sure who put it there, but I think I have a good idea who did, but I just know it wasn't me.

Another interview I remember was of a citizen of Italy who was a drug courier in the Pizza Connection drug investigation of the 70's. He too was found to be deportable from the United States, was taken into custody and returned under escort by our detention and deportation officers to Italy.

From 1990 to 1993, I was assigned to the Worksite Enforcement Unit. In this unit, it was my responsibility, along with others to conduct I-9 (Employment Verification Form), inspections at businesses to determine if a business is hiring illegal aliens to fill jobs that should be filled with authorized workers. I was not really fond of this assignment, but finally gave in and gave it my best.

I was able to identify a lot of businesses, Chinese Restaurants, Meat Packing Plants, Tobacco Farmers, and many other businesses that were constantly filling their workforce with persons from all over the world that were not authorized to be employed in the United States. I applied for and received a lot of Blackie's Inspection Warrants to search businesses for persons not authorized to be employed. A Blackies Inspection Warrant got its name many years ago from a business in the Washington D.C. area known as Blackies House of Beef, which was purported to have illegal aliens employed there and an inspection warrant was obtained to search for illegal aliens working without authorization. Blackies filed a lawsuit to have the warrant quashed and lost their suit and therefor made it possible to obtain this type of warrant. If we wanted to search for documents or other type of evidence, a regular search warrant had to be obtained.

Not only did we conduct business inspections, but we also determined if a business was properly completing the I-9 forms and maintaining the records properly and if they were not, then a monetary fine could be imposed. I, on my own investigation, the biggest fine I had was on a meat packing plant in southern Missouri at $110,000.00. As a co-case agent on another investigation on a business that brought in foreign workers from South Africa as truck drivers the fine was about $320,000.00. I also obtained several seizure warrants and seized a lot of vehicles for violation of Title 8, United States Code, Section 1324, Transporting, Harboring, or Bringing in illegal aliens into the United States. I seized a dump truck, a Cadillac, Volvo, and Tractor Trailer, along with many other types of vehicles. I had seized so many vehicles, that the other agents at the office were teasing me about starting my own car lot. The vehicles were subsequently auctioned off by the United States Marshal Service who handled the disposition of all seized assets.

From 1993 until 1998 I was assigned to a Violent Crimes Gang Joint Task Force at the FBI in Kansas City, Missouri. I really enjoyed this assignment! In the first year, we spent most of our time intelligence gathering. We identified about seventy-five gangs totaling about 1500 member in the Kansas City area. Malditos, 23rd Street Hardcores, 9th Street Dogs, Black Gangster Disciples, Marasalvatruces, just to name a few. We were out riding with local law enforcement patrolling the neighborhoods where these gangs were prevalent. We also identified Asian Gangs, from Vietnam and Cambodia.

In our second year, we began to conduct investigation into the criminal activity of these gangs and were able to develop a lot of investigations that turned into drug investigations and a lot of people were convicted and went to prison for distribution of narcotics, usually along with a weapons violation. When I first became a Special Agent in 1987, INS agents were a part of the Organized Crime Drug Enforcement Task Force or OCDETF. At that time, they were involved in the investigations of the Jamaican Posse or Gangs. These Posses were into cocaine and heroin.

I was taken off the Violent Gang Crime Task Force in 1998 and in 1999 during that year I was the Point of Contact for the Task Force. The Task Force had become involved in an investigation of an elderly woman who was being taken advantage of by a group of fake businesses who promised to do repairs and kept bilking her for money into the tens of thousands. We were sitting in one of her bedrooms watching video of the front door waiting for one of them to return with another scam. Anyway, there were no foreign nationals involved and therefor I could not be involved in the investigation. This was against our agreement as agencies Once again politics came into play, and I was removed from full time participation on the Task Force. It was later in the summer of that year when I was assigned to work the investigation of Serguei.

Remember, Serguei worked and lived in Springfield, Missouri. I was traveling to and from Springfield quite a bit when a job opportunity opened due to the creation of a new office in Springfield, Missouri called a Quick Response Team or a QRT. Our responsibility would be to respond to all call outs from the local law enforcement in the area of our responsibility which covered about twenty-six counties. I enjoyed the Springfield, Missouri area so when the position opened up, I spoke to my wife about the job transfer and move. She agreed so I put in for the position and was accepted to fill one of the vacant positions. I was in Springfield from about 1999 to about 2005.

It was during this time a lot of things began to happen within the INS. I was the Organized Crime, Drug Enforcement Task Force (OCDETF), Point of Contact for our office in Springfield, so any drug investigations that were identified as OCDETF investigations, involving foreign nationals, I was involved in. So, we were conducting fraud investigations, drug investigations, smuggling investigations, you name it we were involved in it!

Chapter Two

The First Investigation 1999-2001

Who is Serguei D. Choukline? What was he doing in the United States, how did he get here, and why was he here? What was his background?

Serguei was born in Khanty-Mansiisk, Russia in 1958. Khanty-Mansiisk is the administrative center, or like our county seat or capitol city, of Khanty-Mansiisk Autonomous Okrug, Russia. It is located on the eastern bank of the Irtysh River about fifteen kilometers (9.3 miles), from its confluence, or joining with the Ob, in the oil-rich region of Western Siberia. From open-source information, Siberia covers about 5.1 million miles and includes about one fifth of the Russian population. I do not know anything of his childhood or his upbringing. I just know about his brief history prior to entering the United States from Russia in 1992 and what we have discovered by his own statements throughout this investigation.

Serguei, in July 1991 was a part of or has claimed that he was a part of or possible leader of a Russian Organized Crime Group or at least wanted his employees to believe. He was purportedly driving home from a bar, after a night out with his friends and other members of the gang. As he passed by a group of individuals on the side of the street, one of them spat on his car. Serguei stopped, backed up and got out of the vehicle. He engaged in an altercation with the person that spat on his car. A fight ensued and Serguei hit the individual in the temporal area on the right side of this person's head, knocking him to the curb to which he subsequently died of his injuries.

In September of 1992, Serguei was arrested by the Russian authorities and interviewed relating to the allegations stemming from the death of the guy he hit, and in October of 1992, Serguei was indicted on the charges of Inflicting Bodily Injury Which Resulted in the Death of Another.

Later in November 1992, Serguei, knowing that charges had been filed in the courts in Russia, fled Russia because he did not want to be taken into custody by Russian authorities.

If you remember, I was assigned to the Springfield, Missouri INS QRT from 1999 to 2005. From late 1998 until 2002, INS and the FBI out of Kansas City, Missouri conducted a joint investigation into the visa fraud activities of Serguei Choukline.

Our first investigation lasted three-years. We were looking into Serguei criminal activity after he entered the United States in November 1992. Serguei entered the United States as a B-1 Visitor for Business which only allowed him to remain in the United States for six months to a year at the most. So, before the end of his authorized stay in the United States when he would have to return to Russia, he changed his status to that of an L1A, Intracompany Transferee.

An L1A Intracompany Transferee (Executive, Managerial) visa, is for "a person who worked for the same subsidiary, or affiliate company for at least one continuous year, (Or 6 months if the company has filed a blanket petition and met the requirements for expedited processing) within the preceding three years in managerial capacity or involving specialized knowledge." Just a wordy way to say that a person who is a representative of a corporation in a foreign country and wants to open a subsidiary business in the United States, they would apply for an L1A Intracompany Transferee Visa to enter the United States to start that business. If the business is successful for a period of three years, the manager can then apply for an E-13, Lawful Permanent Resident status for a Multinational Executive or Manager (slang would be a green card holder).

Once he changed his status from a B-1, Visitor for Business, to that of an L1A Intracompany Transferee, he began to apply for others to enter the United States as an L1A. The others that he began to apply for were his military buddies, people he had served with in the Russian military, helping them flee from, or escape Russia. Serguei used several businesses, which as we determined through our investigation to be fictitious businesses. These businesses were fictitious in that they were businesses in name only and were used for the purpose of providing a business name to put on the applications filed for his friends with fraudulent documents, made up and manufactured to support the visa applications that he had filed on their behalf. If you remember when we spoke to the history of Serguei, we had received information from a source, that he was a Major in Russian Naval Intelligence. It was because of Serguei service in the Russian Military and his position in Naval Intelligence that we contacted the FBI for assistance, wondering if we had a foreign intelligence asset in the United States. The agent's name from the FBI was John, I do not recall his last name.

I had previously worked with the FBI for many years on different gang and narcotics investigations and have even received awards for assisting them in several criminal investigations and for working on and being a member of the Gang Task Force. This time working with the FBI, I was a little bit disappointed. In many instances you will hear of the FBI trying to take over an investigation, not sharing information that they had gathered etc. John and I tried to work this investigation together. Initially, he and I were both working the investigation from Kansas City. After I took the position in Springfield, the investigation continued, but this timed it was him from Kansas City and me from Springfield, Missouri. We were not able to stay in much contact with each other as the investigation continued. We found during this time, that our respective agencies had differences of opinion on how our investigations should be conducted.

John began using his resources at the FBI to find out more about Serguei's background. Because of Serguei's purported or supposed background as an intelligence officer, and our concerns that he may be a Russian military/intelligence asset, John had to really dig deep. If he had found anything along these lines of inquiry to be true, one; he would be unable to share that information with me, and two; the investigation would probably have to be relinquished to the FBI.

I continued to try to identify the people that he had used his fictitious businesses to apply to enter into the United States. I cannot remember the exact number of applicants, but it seems like it was somewhere about fifty.

At the beginning of this investigation, when I was still in the Kansas City Office every Monday morning the Assistant District Director for Investigations (ADDI), would hold a briefing and update us on things going on with other investigations, threats, concerns, just a number of things going on in the area and around the United States within our agency. In this particular Monday's briefing, he identified another Russian Organized Crime investigation going on in and around Seattle, Washington. In that investigation, one of the targets of the organized crime group showed up at the agents front door asking questions. This type of activity conducted by a member of a Russian Organized Crime Group goes to show how bold they could be. It appeared that he was attempting to intimidate the agent and his family. The ADDI advised everyone that I was conducting a similar type of investigation and suggested that we be on the lookout for this type of activity.

It was really weird, because it wasn't but a few days later there were some people of Russia decent, claiming they were selling books in the neighborhood that I lived in. Now I didn't live in Kansas City, I lived in a city outside the city limits of Kansas City, Missouri. One of these individuals of Russian descent, showed up at my door trying to sell children's books. It really gave me and my family an uneasy feeling as my wife took care of a couple of our grandchildren and they were present at our home that day. I told him that I didn't have any children and about that time, our granddaughter looked out the side window, next to the front door and was waving at me. He said, "Well who is that?" I told him that my wife baby sat a couple of children once in a while and told him the next-door neighbor had children. I checked with the city that I lived in and the people selling the books did go through the proper procedures and obtained a license to sell in the neighborhood, but then I wonder did they give their true names or was it a cover. If Serguei is in Russian Military Intelligence, he would certainly have the ability to set this up. I think you will agree by the end of this investigation. That will always be a wonder for me. I reported the information to my ADDI, and he passed it along to the other agents in the office and up the chain of command should I have any future visits from Russians.

I had developed a source of information (Source), that had been contacted by Serguei for the purposes of supplying information for his writing of a book on Russian Organized Crime and gangs in Russia and in the United States. I will not identify this person as he had a pretty important position himself at his place of employment, but I will say that he was a retired United States Army Intelligence officer with a substantial rank, so he knew the kinds of questions to ask and things to look for as he dealt with Serguei.

This Source met with Serguei several times at restaurants and nightclubs as well as at his [Serguei's] home to discuss his background in Russian Organized Crime and how he was able to assist in drafting a book as it relates to this subject, and Serguei did like to brag about himself and his accomplishments. This Source was also able to conduct some analysis of Serguei which basically said Serguei was narcissistic and loved to talk about himself, which as I said, appears to be the case.

It was through this Source who because he had been to Serguei's residence to discuss his potential book, that I was able to get a drawn diagram that he had completed of the interior of Serguei's home which will become important during our second investigation of Serguei Choukline. He is also the person who first saw a photograph of Serguei in military uniform with Boris Yeltsin and identified him with the rank of Major in the Russian Naval Intelligence.

Serguei, as I stated earlier, created fictitious businesses and business addresses which were the addresses he used on the applications for his L1A applicants. Some of these addresses, as we continued with our investigation, were given as the mailing address for the businesses were subsequently determined to be a Post Office or Drop Boxes at a Mailbox Etcetera. If there was a street address listed on the application as the actual street location of the business, these were determined to be addresses that Serguei knew to people that lived there, or they were addresses where he had previously resided or just addresses that he had passed by and wrote down.

It worked like this! Think of a spider web, as this is the best way I can describe it. In the center of the web where you might find the spider, put Serguei's name in a circle. As you expand out to the next junction, list the drop or mail box in the drop box circle. Go around Serguei's name and put about six boxes. I think he had about eight, but to be conservative, put six. In these boxes were the mail drop boxes. In these next circles, we will put the name of the fictitious business which are supposed to have these drop box as its mailing address. There might be two or three circles to each box at this junction due to the number of businesses he had. Now, on the next junction out beyond the businesses, we will list the names of people other than Serguei that had access to each business. So, it has now really expanded out. This is what we were dealing with. If you don't know it, when a person rents a drop box or mail box like this, they have to fill out a Postal Service form which identifies who has access to each mail box and their actual physical address where the business is located. If you remember the definition of an L1A Intracompany Transferee, the position was for a manager's or an executive's position. Each person that was listed as having access to pick up mail from these drop boxes/mail boxes were identified as an Executive or Manager of the listed business that Serguei had applied for.

The applications filed, identified these addresses that Serguei falsified on the applications as the actual business address from which he submitted doctored photographs with the applications to make it appear that these were offices located at each location with persons working in the offices. As I said, these office addresses were actually houses rented at one time by Serguei or were associated with someone he knew or met in several cities around Joplin, Missouri, Carl Junction, Missouri and Webb City, Missouri.

We or I, since John from the FBI was in Kansas City and working other intelligence related investigations, conducted a lot of surveillance and interviewed the actual residents of the addresses provided by Serguei as a place of business for these fictitious companies that these L1A Intra Company Transferees worked. One address that I specifically remember, and I do not know why a big yellow house on North Moffet Avenue in Joplin, Missouri that belonged to a doctor that Serguei had met a few times. It was a big three-story house, and the driveway went down either behind or beside the house. I interviewed the owner of the residence during this investigation who stated that Serguei never lived there but he had met Serguei. Serguei having visited the owner of the residence, decided to use the address for one of his businesses. There were many such addresses that were checked and determined to be never lived in or owned by Serguei. I still do not know how he was able to get some of these addresses other than just drive by them and write them down.

Serguei Choukline became involved with a female Russian by the name of Elena Moshennika. Not in a romantic relationship, but a business relationship. They were not involved in the L1A visa fraud scam together, but a collateral scheme and money-making scam he and she were running to make money off of Russian and American families. This was done by bringing children of purported Russian Police Officer to visit and live with American families in the area of Joplin and Nevada, Missouri. Elena was also trying to bring foreign students into the United States to attend college in Joplin, Missouri and Neosho, Missouri area.

It was determined through our investigation that Elena had made some arrangement with the Dean of Students at the college to allow them access to and the ability to attend the University. It was all a scam to cheat the purported student out of more money, finding out once they arrived in the United

States, they would have to pay more fees like rent, insurance, and transportation. I attempted to interview her several times, but she would not speak to me. A good friend of Elena was Tatiana Pomoshchnika who was also involved in the student visa fraud scheme. Pomoshchnika was finally interviewed as it relates to Moshennika but there was never enough information obtained to pursue criminal charges.

Moshennika had a boyfriend Andrei Tretiakov. Tretiakov had been petitioned by Serguei Choukline as an L1A Intracompany Transferee for one of the fictitious businesses known as Worldwide Intelligence Corporation. This company was the only company that Serguei Choukline himself, and a person known a John Irish purportedly ran. This business actually had no function! It was a business in name only. Serguei Choukline and John Irish did have business cards made up to impress others by giving out cards but there was no functioning business operation. Irish was a Martial Arts Instructor in Joplin, Missouri. He not only held classes at his martial arts studio, but he did teach self-defense to new students in attendance at the Police Academy in Joplin held at the University.

As I said as it relates to Worldwide Intelligence Corporation, Serguei and Irish went into this business together, but it never grew to anything. It was for nothing but show. However, both Serguei Choukline and John Irish were interviewed as it relates to the visa application filed on behalf of Andre Tretiakov by Worldwide Intelligence Corporation. Serguei and Irish both denied ever having filed an application for him and denied the signature on the application form belonged to either of them. Tretiakov was subsequently arrested at his place of employment, a Trucking Company in Strafford, Missouri and was one of the many that were placed in removal proceedings and deported from the United States.

Serguei, in his attempt to influence others, created another fictitious business identified as International Advisory Board on Organized Crime and Terrorism, using his business address as 1304 East Republic Road, Suite 141, Springfield, Missouri, 65804 which was later identified as a Mail Drop Box. He also created a business called Russian Standard Ltd., 305 East Walnut Street, Suite 110A, Springfield, Missouri 65806 (we want to remember this address), in the name of Gregory Temkin, whom we never met, and SDI Worldwide Intelligence, Division of Special Investigations, Dr. Serguei D. Choukline, Rt 3, Box 829-9, Joplin, Missouri 64802, all of which were subsequently identified as mail drop boxes except for the Walnut address in Springfield, Missouri.

Another person associated with Serguei Choukline, and Elena Moshennika was Pavel Doulov. He too received an L1A Intracompany Transferee Visa through Serguei. Several attempts were made to interview him, but he was never at home. An investigative report was completed and submitted to the Examinations Section (Citizenship and Immigration Services today) to place him in removal proceedings for visa fraud. It is still unknown whether he was removed from the United States or not.

In late December of 1999, just before Christmas, Lilia, one of agents in the Springfield, Missouri QRT Office was the duty agent for that day and had received a call from the

Department of Revenue Driver License Office in downtown Springfield, Missouri. The caller stated that there were six individuals believed to be from Russia, with one of them acting as a translator for the others attempting to get driver licenses and they were still in the office.

Lilia was sent with one of the other agents to the Driver License Office to interview these individuals and determine their status in the United States. Even though I had the investigation going against Serguei and knew a lot of the names of the Russians in the area, I was not sent. Upon arrival at the license office, Lilia interviewed them, obtained their addresses, place of employment etc. and called the office to have the names checked and, in the meantime, released them to go on their way as it appeared at first glance their statuses were good. However, when she called the office and spoke to the Supervisory Special Agent, she mentioned Serguei Choukline's name. He told her to return to the office and to get with me with the information that she had obtained from the six individuals she interviewed.

After Lilia returned to the Office and made contact with me, it was determined that we needed to go to their residence and conduct a more in-depth interview of them as from Lilia's notes, it was indeed Serguei Choukline, and these foreign nationals were working in the hotel/motel industry. So, Lilia and I departed in my vehicle and traveled to the address they provided to her at the driver license office. Upon our arrival at the address of 318 North Hampton, Unit B, Springfield, Missouri we observed the six foreign nationals exiting their vehicle and walking toward the apartment. Since there were six of them and only two of us, I called the office for a couple of Detention Officers to meet Lilia and I at this location. After a short time, Cliff, 6'3" about 300 lbs. and another detention officer arrived in a detention van. We also called for assistance from the Springfield, Missouri Police Department to meet us to stand by while we conducted further interviews of these individuals.

After everyone arrived, we knocked on the door of the identified apartment and was met at the door by Michael Siminov, a citizen of a country near Russia. Michael is the person that was acting as the translator at the driver license office. We identified ourselves at the door as agents with INS and asked if we could come in and ask them further questions about their status in the United States and their employment. Michael invited us in and since he spoke English, he assisted us in conducting our interviews. After speaking to each of the six and actually seeing their documentation in the apartment, it was determined that all of them were out of status and were taken into custody. There was Michael and his girlfriend Darla, an Armenian pilot with his adult son, two men from the country of Georgia, Givi and Zurabi and a Russian by the name of Maksimov. All were transported back to the Springfield INS office and placed in removal proceedings. Since Michael is the signor on the apartment lease, before we departed the apartment, we asked for his consent to search the apartment, which he provided. A search of the apartment revealed pay stubs and other documentation indicating that they were working for Serguei Choukline.

While we were at the Springfield INS Office completing the paperwork to place these six individuals in removal proceedings, Michael kept looking my way and motioned for me to come over to him. I asked if everything was okay, he said yes and then said "I think you want to speak to me" I asked why is that? He stated, "Because I have more information about Serguei!" So, I spoke further with him, and he provided information about Serguei's new business adventure of bringing people into the United States to work in the hotel/motel industry and began to inform me of how he treated his employees such as putting his girlfriend in this apartment with 5 other men, 4 of whom she did not know. He stated that she was a single girl and should not be in that situation. He stated that he and Serguei did not get along and that he had almost come to blows with Serguei.

Michael informed us that Serguei had used his Social Security Number and name to rent this duplex. Michael informed me that the actual rent of the duplex is only $500.00 per month but charged each of them $400.00 each. Since there were a total of eight people living in the duplex that came to about $3,200.00, that put about $2,700.00 in Serguei's pocket every month, just from this one group. Serguei's use of Michael's Social Security Number and name was beneficial to us at the time, because Michael was able to sign the Consent to Search the duplex allowing us to locate the documents and evidence we were able to get and use in our investigation.

Michael, of course not his true name was given the opportunity to become an Informant, which he did and was subsequently released on his own recognizance. The others were also placed in removal proceedings and given an immigration bond. Michael later posted Darla's bond and she too was released pending an immigration hearing.

Just a few months later, we were prepared to present Serguei for prosecution for the L1A visa fraud. The visa applications for the L1A Intracompany Transferee were sent from Serguei's residence in Springfield, Missouri to an attorney in New York, who then filed the application with the INS Service Center in Lincoln, Nebraska. As we filed our affidavit for a warrant and charges for Serguei, it was determined that INS was its own worst enemy.

In filing a prosecution such as this, documenting the mailings is important to pursue a charge of Mail Fraud, in violation of 18 U.S.C. Section 1341 which basically states, that a person used or caused to be used, the United States Postal System to mail the fraudulent and falsified applications for L1A Visa Applications, to obtain visas for people he has induced to come to and remain in the United States and work for his service-oriented business. So, how were we our own worst enemy? The Service Center in Lincoln, Nebraska in each of the application filings failed to maintain the original of, or a copy of the envelope to show the mailings crossed state lines to further evidence of the mail fraud.

Therefore, the United States Attorney's office, even though we were able to document the fictitious businesses, drop boxes, doctored photographs, interviews, and arrests, felt that they were unable to properly pursue prosecution without the mail fraud charge and declined to proceed further. Since INS had arrested many of the individuals that had been applied for who would have been potential witnesses and they had now been placed in removal proceedings for deportation, and many of which had already been removed from the United States, depleted the witness pool as well. Michael, our informant that had been developed, was just a little too late in the making, and since he had a falling out with Serguei, it was more difficult for him to gather information to help with this particular prosecution.

Serguei fled to Russia in about 2000 in an attempt to avoid arrest by INS on Administrative violations for his own visa fraud and criminal charges for the L1A Intracompany Transferee visa fraud scheme he was involved in. He was running scared! Though the criminal charges against Serguei were no longer a threat to be prosecuted for, he still had the immigration charges for visa fraud looming over his head. He, for whatever reason, thought it safer to return to Russia to possibly face the charge of murder in Russia. Makes no sense to me, but that was his decision.

Serguei was married to Irina A. Choukline also a citizen of Russian, now a Naturalized Citizen of the United States, and had a son, Serguei Choukline Jr., a citizen and national by birth in the United States. Serguei Choukline Jr. was a student in school when all of this began. Irina was a nurse at a Hospital in Springfield, Missouri. Serguei knew that he was wanted in Russia for the previous killing of an individual and could not take the chance of his wife and son being taken into custody for any reason if they traveled with him, after all they were United States citizens, so he left them behind in the United States not knowing for sure how long he was going to be gone, in custody or if he was going to prison.

In 2000 after his return to Russia, Serguei was indeed arrested on the outstanding warrant for the previous charge of Infliction of Bodily Injury Which Caused the Death of Another and remained in custody in a Russian jail in Arkhangelsk, Russia for a period of about 11 months until his court date in May 2001.

Serguei was eventually prosecuted for the offense, and was convicted in 2001 in Arkhangelsk, Russia for the offense of Causing the Death of Another by Negligence, a lesser charge, in violation of Section 109.1 and was sentenced to three years in prison. Unconfirmed information indicates that Serguei paid about $50,000.00 to be granted amnesty for the offense. This is information that was provided by a Russian News Paper, three years after the conviction.

The Russian News Article, titled "American Werewolf," published in the Premiere News Paper, in Vologda, Russia, dated March 10, 2004, written by an unknown author detail who Serguei was, the crime he committed, how he fled Russia, his return, and his conviction and release. It was translated on Google Translate but was not in very good English. I have attempted to summarize the article but cover the details in, hopefully, better English.

The article states as follows:

"Vologda Police helped solve a high-profile criminal case in the Arkhangelesk Region." Serguei Choukline (Shuklin), who was a Deputy City Council Member from the city of Severodvinsk and suspected of murder had been a fugitive for ten years. Shuklin, has popped up in America and has now been seen in the city of Vologda.

Shuklin had been seen in the Spasskaya hotel and was working as a commercial director. Shuklin in the early 1990's when the cooperative movement began to emerge, Shuklin who was just over thirty years of age quickly became involved with the influential and the richest people in Severodvinsk and headed a company called the "Trade House" and was elected to the position of a Deputy City Council Member. All of this changed.

Shuklin later became involved in an altercation. The incident was explained in an article in the Northern Rabochiy newspaper, written by Olga Ovchinnkova, a journalist, who said the car that Shuklin and some of his friends were in was stopped by several guys and after a short skirmish, Shuklin hit one of the persons in the altercation after he spat on Serguei's car, this individual fell to the ground and hit his head on the curb, and later died.

After the initiation of a criminal proceeding, Severodvinsk prosecutors' office refused to issue a sanction (warrant), against Shuklin for his arrest after the altercation. Shuklin, without waiting for a trial, packed up his family and moved to Joplin, Missouri.

For a long time Shuklin had not been heard from until the head of the Department of Internal Affairs of the Arkhangelsk Region, General Okhrimenko paid a working visit to the United States in 1997. The Joplin Globe Newspaper said that the guest's visit from Russia, was organized by Sergei Shuklin.

This information was very upsetting to the citizens of Arkhangelsk, stating it was like "Thunder in the Sky," a criminal wanted on suspicions of murder meets with General Okhrimenko the head of the regional police department in America! Later, General Okhrimenko repeatedly said that Shuklin had nothing to do with his trip to the States."

About a year later, a person known as John Irish (Irish from our first investigation), Chief Instructor of the Missouri Police Academy arrived in Arkhangelsk on a return visit and the authorities asked for his assistance in having Shuklin returned to Russia.

At the end of 2000, the fugitive returned to Russia on his own. Evidently, he thought the criminal case was forgotten and there was no evidence.

However, according to journalist Olga Ovchinnikova, Shuklin came to Russia voluntarily, without the intervention of American authorities. Only Shuklin did not go to his native city of Arkhangelsk, but to Vologda.

The head of the search department of the Vologda Regional Police, Department of Internal Affairs Yuri Mokievsky, found that Shuklin was residing in the Spasskaya Hotel and also working again as a Commercial Director. After receiving their briefing, the officers went to the hotel to arrest Shuklin.

Mokievsky said they were preparing for any resistance because Arkhangelsk reported that Shuklin is either a boxer or has hand-to-hand combat skills. They encountered Serguei in the hotel, and he was very cooperative. They escorted him to his room and waited for him to pack his things, and then escorted him to the second police department and then to Arkhangelsk.

The whole of Severodvinsk watched the trial for several months. Ten years after the fight, the main suspect was in the dock (in custody). By that time, there were only a few witnesses left. Some of the witnesses were dead and some had left Severodvinsk. The judge who initially accepted the case has now passed away.

It was not possible to find out who struck the fatal blow that evening. Shuklin was subsequently found guilty under Article 109 of the Criminal Code of the Russian Federation (Causing death by negligence) and was sentenced to three years in prison and was to serve his sentence in a settlement colony. However, he was granted amnesty and released in the courtroom.

Shuklin was also given a travel ban, not allowed to leave the country. Shuklin did not appeal the conviction or the verdict and a week later, left for the United States again and in that same month May of 2001, Shuklin reentered the United States.

It had been determined that Serguei had obtained his initial visa by fraud. How did he commit visa fraud? After Serguei was indicted on the initial charge in Russia of Inflicting Bodily Injury Which Resulted in the Death of Another he applied for and received a B-1 Visitor for Business Visa before there was an outcome of the case in Russia. The indictment was still in effect.

If any of you know of anyone or have helped anyone complete a visa application to enter the United States know there is a question on the application that asks if you have ever been arrested, charged, or indicted for a felony. Since Serguei's initial response to that question was no and the application was filed after his arrest and indictment, Serguei withheld a material fact in an application and had therefore made a false statement on the application for his visa thus committing visa fraud.

Serguei was a tough individual! He was a purported member/leader of a Russian Organized Crime Group, that is, by his own statements to his employees, but before that, he was a Major in Russian Naval Intelligence, reported by sources to have been assigned to submarines. At one point in time, there was a photograph seen in his home of him in military uniform standing next to Boris Yeltsin, the once president of the Russian Federation. Serguei at one time claimed to the people that worked for him to be the mayor of Arkhangelsk, Oblast, Russia which is on the White Sea in the Northern Region of Russia. Based on the news article from Russia, Serguei was not the mayor of Arkhangelsk, but a Deputy City Council Member of Severodvinsk. In this position he evidently had the opportunity to have in his possession verification ink stamps that were used for approvals of certificates. It will be explained a little later in the book why this is important.

Serguei was subsequently arrested in the United States in 2002 on the administrative charge of visa fraud in violation of Section 212(a)(6)(c)(i) of the Immigration and Nationality Act (INA), "Misrepresentation", which states "IN GENERAL. – Any alien who, by fraud or willfully misrepresenting a material fact, seeks to procure (or has sought to procure or has procured) a visa, other documentation, or admission into the United States or other benefits provided under this Act is inadmissible." In other words, Serguei was inadmissible at the time he entered the United States and should not have been allowed entry and was therefore excludable from the United States.

Serguei was charged administratively with this allegation, was arrested by me at his home in Springfield,

Missouri and he was later released on a $10,000.00 immigration bond. Yes, foreign nationals who enter the United States have, if charged and placed in removal proceedings have the right to an administrative hearing and a bond. Serguei posted the $10,000.00 and was released from custody.

What I did find out later is that my co-case agent with the FBI, who without my knowledge, was going to offer Serguei the opportunity to become a source of information for them. We are supposed to be co-case agents, but information sharing evidently was not a part of that in this case. I will state that I don't know if this was John's decision, or the decision of his superiors. In any governmental operation, no matter what agency you are a part of, upper-level management make decisions that the agent may or may not agree with. The agent then has to make all of the apologies make it sound like they are in concurrence, hope for the best and move on. However, I beat them to the draw on this one, since I had arrested Serguei and placed him in administrative removal proceedings, they could not pursue him as a source and therefore had to withdraw any offers that had been made to him.

Unfortunately, and there is always an unfortunately, INS Legal got involved and determined that since Serguei was convicted of a lesser charge of death by negligence, which in the United States is equivalent to a lesser charge of Involuntary Manslaughter, is not a deportable offense. He was then granted amnesty while still in the courtroom! It was like nothing had happened. He is no longer deportable from the United States. Therefore, the administrative charges against Serguei for visa fraud were dismissed and his $10,000.00 bond was returned.

Since the United States Attorney's Office declined to prosecute, and Serguei was determined to no longer be deportable after his conviction in Russia since it had been reduced to our version of Involuntary Manslaughter, a non-deportable offense, our investigation into the criminal activity and immigration violations of Serguei Choukline was over, cases are now closed.

Chapter Three

The In-Between Case Period 2001-2004

My first investigations of Serguei were shut down. Since the investigations were now closed, life as a criminal investigator doesn't stop, we move on to other cases, projects, details, whatever the agency decides. We don't have time to ponder on any particular investigation, wonder what I could have done better, what did I do wrong, was it my fault, was it someone else's fault etc., etc., etc. As I said in the last chapter, we at INS were our own worst enemy in that the Service Center in Lincoln, NE did not keep the envelopes to show the mailings from Springfield to New York to Lincoln, NE so the United States Attorney didn't want to continue on with the investigation and decided not to pursue charges against Serguei.

So, I did write an email to the Fraud Investigator at the Service Center in Lincoln, NE. for him to share with his superiors and the staff. I laid out in detail what the element of the crime were and why it was so important for the Examiners/Adjudicators assigned to review and approve the applications at the Service Center to keep everything that comes with the application to include the envelope that the application was sent in. The Fraud Investigator did indeed share my email with the powers that be in the Service Center, and he provided me a copy of the email that went out across the Service Center directing all Examiners/Adjudicators to keep copies of all documents including envelopes as they review the applications that are received at the Service Center. So, I guess I did do some good, and hopefully this type of problem will not occur in any future investigations.

Did the Assistant United States Attorney, or his office use this as an excuse to get out of prosecuting Serguei? I don't think so! I have worked with them many times, and I believe they would have told me why and for what reason they declined to pursue prosecution and I believe that was the case in this instance.

On September 11, 2001, only a few months after the investigations closed, we were all moving on with our lives when at about 8:00 AM, I was in Bolivar, Missouri buying a new truck, and we all know what happened on that date. We, the United States was attacked by 19 cowardly terrorist who attacked the Twin Towers in New York City, the Pentagon in Washington, D.C., and the crash of Flight 93 that crashed in a field in Pennsylvania. My cell phone rang, and all leave was canceled, and I was to get back to the office as soon as I could. I took my wife's car and returned home and picked up my government vehicle and went to work. My wife stayed at the dealership and signed all of the paperwork for the truck and drove it home. That turned in to about a sixteen-hour day!

We spent the next few months working with other agencies to identify persons with possible terrorist connections and foreign students that were out of status that may be in our area of operation, locating and arresting them for violation of their status i.e., overstay student, out of status visitor. If they were out of status, they were arrested and placed in removal proceedings. Typical government operation to work on crisis management. Don't worry about it until something bad happens. September 11 was certainly something bad that happened.

On one particular day in October or November of 2001, then Senator Kit Bond of Missouri, traveled to all of the INS Offices in the State of Missouri. He was meeting with the Special Agents in the different offices of Kansas City, Missouri, St. Louis, Missouri and Springfield, Missouri asking the agents what we could have done better to have protected ourselves from the events of September 11, 2001. The Supervisor, Randy, and several Special Agents to include me, John, and Lilia from the Springfield, Missouri QRT were asked to meet with him when he came to our office.

It was a true honor to meet Senator Bond and I have the photograph that was taken with him on the day of the meeting hanging on the wall in my home office today. He asked all of the right questions about background checks, better tracking of a student once the enter the United States. Random checks on their sponsor and reported address where they were to be living and pursue removal proceedings if they do not report a change of address. The meeting was only a couple of hours long, and I remember the Senator had a bad cold, but he felt these meetings that were scheduled with the three INS offices in the State of

Missouri were important enough to follow through with. We saw some changes occur over the years, but certainly not enough and not quick enough.

In December of 2001, there was an email request for volunteers to go on detail to D.C. to be assigned to the Office of Internal Audit or OIA starting in the beginning of 2002 for a period of one year. OIA is the equivalent of conducting Internal Affairs investigations with a local police department. I spoke to Randy, the Supervisory Special Agent in Springfield, Missouri and asked for his blessing on submitting my name to be considered for the detail. He approved and sent the request up to Kansas City and I was later accepted to fill the detailed position. The Springfield, Missouri QRT fell under the operational authority of the Kansas City, Missouri INS Office. So, if we needed approvals for any operations or funds, request for training or special details such as this one the request had to go through Kansas City.

In January 2002, I began the detail to HQ/OIA in Washington, D.C. as I said, it was for a period of one year conducting internal investigations. Though this detail was under the supervision of HQ/OIA I worked out of my home office in Springfield, Missouri, this was my home base. I initially travelled to HQ/OIA for some training and equipment then returned to the Springfield QRT Office. HQ/OIA authorized me to work out of my home because of the sensitivity of these types of investigations. The only time we came into the office was for supplies and to complete our pay voucher. Anytime I traveled to conduct an investigation within the OIA, it was all planned by me without the knowledge of my District Office or the Springfield Office.

The ADDI in Kansas City, Missouri did not like me working from home as I was authorized to by HQ/OIA. He called my supervisor and complained about the time-keeping and whatever else it was that he complained about, and my supervisor called me at home and told me of the ADDI's concerns and wishes. He did not want me working out of my home. He needed to know what I was doing. I had to contact my detail supervisor about the ADDI's issues. My detail supervisor very diplomatically said "Your ADDI knows you work for me over this next year, and he really can't control this situation. However, you have to return to work for him when this detail is over. I will go along with whatever you feel you need to do!" So, I thought about it a little and decided it would be better if I went along with my ADDI and agreed to work out of the office, but I needed space that I could secure. So, the ADDI instructed my supervisor to allow me to use one of our interview rooms in the Springfield QRT to use as an office, put a padlock on the door and give me the keys. Therefore, it would be secured from access by any of the other agents and this would meet the requirement to secure the files as these were considered sensitive investigations.

I traveled all over the southern United States primarily conducting internal investigations of complaints against Border Patrol Agents for excessive use of force, Immigration inspectors for theft of alien property/money, detention officers for preferential treatment of inmates and or their attorneys, allowing special access to their clients. All kinds of allegations of misconduct by an officer.

What was interesting though, is the fact that through all the statistics that were gathered up to this point in time, regarding these types of investigations, 96% of all allegations against agents, be it Border Patrol Agents, Special Agents, Inspectors, or Examiners whoever it is, were determined to be false allegations. They were usually based on vengeance, retribution or whatever the case, just to get back at the individual officer or agency. Of all the investigations that I conducted over six months, I only found two or three where the agent or agency appeared to be at fault.

However, politics are still at play, even on the lower levels. As it says, "it all rolls downhill." Evidently, the District Director of the Kansas City office at the time, did not want to approve my request for the detail to Headquarters. Which I did not know. The District Director and the ADDI and my supervisor, the Supervisory Special Agent of the Springfield, Missouri QRT Office had differences of opinion of whether I should be sent on this detail or not. So, what happened? The ADDI took it upon himself to submit my name without the authorization of the District Director, and I was accepted to participate in the detail, and he was livid!

It caused all kinds of riffs such as having the padlocked office instead of working from home which was authorized by D.C. They didn't have control over my comings and goings without their knowledge or where I was going. No control over my activity. Finally, I gave in. I spoke to my detail supervisor in D.C. and withdrew from the detail and returned to my normal duties in the Springfield, Missouri QRT just 6 months into a one-year detail. I was however able to continue to use my padlocked office for a couple of years longer and not have to return to the cubicle I once occupied. This was in July of 2002.

In February of 2003, I was sent once again to Washington, D.C. on detail to the National Security Group to assist in the further identification of foreign nationals in the United States that were subject to interviews by the FBI and INS. This was a rotating detail and agents were sent at random from around the country to participate in the ongoing operation. I remember we, my wife and I had traveled from Springfield, Missouri to Kansas City, Missouri to attend the retirement party of the District Director on our way to D.C. He was one of those that was not happy with the upcoming merger into the Department of Homeland Security and wanted to retire before it took place. We, my wife, and I, left that night after the retirement dinner for the District Director, thinking we could drive as far as St. Louis, stay overnight there and hopefully a snowstorm that was coming through would pass by and we would be at the tail end of it. We woke the next morning in St. Louis to find that that was not the case, the storm was slower than we thought, and we ended up driving all the way to Washington, D.C. in four-wheel drive with the snow storm overhead. We were in D.C. for 30 days.

After I returned from this detail to Washington, D.C., I returned to my normal duties in Springfield, MO. Over the next year or so, we worked closely with the local law enforcement agencies in our 26-county area of operation. I began teaching classes at the local Police Academy and giving classes to local law enforcement agencies trying to describe ways that we could all work together to identify criminal aliens that had moved into the area of southwest Missouri. I was still the OCDETF Coordinator for our small QRT Office. As I mentioned in Chapter One, if there was a drug investigation ongoing that involved foreign nationals, most of the time we had an agent involved and then I became involved as the coordinator to attempt to get funding for our agents. I remember in March of 2003 going to Kansas City to attend an OCDETF Coordinators meeting to present an investigation that our Springfield Office was involved in to get approval for it to be an OCDETF investigation, which the committee did approve, and a request for additional funding from the Department of Justice' OCDETF funding was subsequently approved as well.

Part of our duties of the QRT was as I said to respond to local law enforcement when they requested assistance. This request could come at all hours of the day or night. There were times, when I was called out for a smuggling load (A load of illegal aliens being transported across the United States), enroute to various locations to look for work, or meet family members who were already present in the United States. If I was the duty agent, I was definitely going to get called. If a smuggling load were encountered, we would all get called out eventually. Most of the people we encountered in these smuggling loads were of Hispanic descent and to communicate with them, we had to speak Spanish.

At the time, my Spanish was pretty decent. When I went through the Federal Law Enforcement Training Center (FLETC), in Brunswick, GA., I was put in the Native Speaker Class for Spanish Language training. That happened because I had been in the agency for a while and my Spanish was okay as a Detention Officer, and one of the Senior Special Agents from

Kansas City was a detailed Spanish instructor at the academy when I started. I think he had something to do with me being put at that higher level. He emphatically denied having anything to do with it, with a big smile on his face, but I'm still not sure I believed him. I myself don't think I should have been put there, because I had to work twice as hard as anyone to get through the class. Maybe that was his reason if he was behind it. Our Spanish training during this time was the entire 5 months or so of training and we had five Spanish test through the five-month period. I graduated with and 92.4 percent average in Spanish. I was pretty excited about that final score because I truly did work very hard to get through this class.

So, back to our QRT duties, if we were called out many times I was asked to speak to the driver of the vehicle and conduct the more in-depth interviews of the passengers in an attempt to get them to identify the driver or smuggler in that particular group. I had a fairly good record with either breaking the driver or getting someone to identify him. The driver would also be presented for prosecution for transporting illegal aliens in violation of Title 8, United States Code, Section 1324(a)(1)(A)(ii), Transporting Illegal Aliens in the United States in furtherance of a violation of law.

We had to not only respond to law enforcement for smuggling of aliens, but aliens smuggling narcotics and monies. We were called out many times with the Missouri States Highway Patrol and the Drug Enforcement Administration (DEA) to determine the status of the alien transporting the drugs and money and to be able to put a detainer on that person so they could not post bond and abscond.

I remember one specific time that Erik, one of the agents in Springfield, responded to a callout by the Missouri Highway Patrol and the DEA who had stopped a vehicle on Interstate 44. The driver of the vehicle was transporting a large sum of money toward the southern border. A drug dog sniffed the money and of course it alerted to narcotics. I don't remember where I heard it, but I have heard that with any large amount of money, a drug dog will be able to detect narcotics. Anyway, the dog alerted, and the funds were seized by the DEA. Erik arrested the driver who was illegally present in the United States and brought him back to the now Springfield HSI office to be interviewed. Since the driver spoke English, Erik conducted the interview himself. During the interview, he was told by the driver, that the money that was seized by the DEA, was actually proceeds from the smuggling of illegal aliens into the United States. Based on this statement, Erik went to the United States Attorney's Office and obtained a Seizure Warrant for the money and served it on the DEA. The money was then transferred to the Department of Homeland Security for Asset Forfeiture. The DEA was not happy, but it was not drug proceeds but alien smuggling proceeds and that needed to be accurately documented.

The informant that I developed in the first investigation of Serguei was still working for me in the capacity of an informant. In fact, he was really doing a good job. He and his now wife worked several different jobs to make ends meet. His wife, Darla was working in the restaurant industry as a waitress and decided that she too wanted to become and informant as she encountered a lot of information through her work that would be beneficial in a criminal investigation, or just information in general. So now, both of them were providing me information. There was no financial benefit to either Michael or Darla for their work in this capacity. They enjoyed the ability to give back. They were taken away from the threats of Serguei and I think they enjoyed the mystery of the work also. But they did get the opportunity to remain in the United States while waiting for the decision in their own applications for benefit.

As I said, I think they just wanted to give back. They kept trying, as per their culture, to give me gifts. I had to continuously decline what they were trying to give. There was a painting, wine from their home country, a couple of other things that I don't remember. I had a hard time making them understand that I could not accept their gifts in the capacity that they were in as informants. I know it offended them at first, but when I was finally able to explain the type of relationship that we had to maintain because it could cost me my job, then they finally understood and complied.

One meeting that I had with Michael, he was the one that asked to meet me. That usually only happened if he had information to give me as an informant. I was really busy that day and didn't have the time to spare and was going to ask to meet later. Then he proceeded to tell me he and Darla were having some marital issues and was asking for advise! So, I made the time and went to meet him. Now I am no counselor of any kind, marriage or otherwise. But I am a Christian and I know that God's instruction for marriage is clearly laid out in the Bible. I discussed scripture with Michael, and he rededicated his life to Christ as his Lord and Savior. He was so excited that he called Darla and she came to meet us at the restaurant in

Springfield where he and I were meeting. I discussed scripture with her as well, and she too rededicated her life to Christ as her Lord and Savior. The outcome of our meeting was certainly not what I expected, especially since I was hesitant to meet in the first place. You are always careful how close you get to an informant as I previously discussed, because you never know if they have an alternative reason for taking on this position. There are certain instructions and protocols within the agency about personal relationships and involvement with informants especially while they are working for you. To see them both, rededicate their lives to Christ was a blessing to me. A blessing that only another Christian will understand. To know that anyone will spend eternity in heaven is a blessing beyond understanding to a non-Christian. Our personal relationship has now taken on a new meaning. I found out later that Darla accepted Christ at the age of 15 and was baptized the same day, and Michael accepted Christ at the age of 6, but wasn't baptized until the age of 25. After we discussed the biblical principles of marriage, it was felt they were going to work very hard to save their marriage.

Michael, called me on another day this time saying that he had information on a document vendor from Cuba who lived in the Springfield, Missouri area. Michael stated that he and Darla had just moved into an apartment in Springfield, Missouri and were approached by the front gate security officer who found out they were from another country and asked if they had work authorization in the United States. Michael told him he did not, and this Cuban told him that he could get him a fake work authorization card.

We presented the information to the United States Attorney in Springfield, Missouri and he agreed to prosecute if we got the evidence we needed. We wired Michael with a consensually monitored recorder (in other words, Michael agreed to be wired), and sent him to meet the Cuban. We were on the outside providing security and surveillance and were ready to go in and rescue Michael if the Cuban figured out that Michael was wired. The Cuban spoke clearly about the documents, how much they would cost and how long it would take to get them. We did this a couple of times, and on the day, he was to produce the fraudulent documents, we surveilled him all over the city. He called Michael and informed him that he had the documents. We contacted the United States Attorney and obtained a Federal Search warrant for his residence, we entered with the warrant and recovered the documents and several others, along with the money used to pay for the documents. He was telling Michael he was getting the documents from someone else, when in actuality, he was making them himself. The Cuban was subsequently arrested and charged with producing fraudulent immigration documents and was sentenced to several years' probation and did not have to go to prison but was still convicted as a felon. The Cuban said at the end of everything, "You guys are good, you got me!"

Another time, Michael contacted me, he was delivering Pizza, and one of his deliveries took him to the apartment of a person that Michael knew had committed a crime and was wanted by the Greene County, Missouri Sheriff's Department in Springfield. This person, who was from the middle east, even invited Michael to his apartment to share a dinner with.

Michael stated that it was different, because they used their hands to eat, everyone from the same big dish. Anyway, Michael called me and told me where the middle easterner was living, what apartment he was in and what kind of car he was driving. I went to the address in Springfield, Missouri that was given to me by Michael and surveilled the address. When I saw him arrive, I called the Sheriff's Department and identified myself and explained that I received the information from a verified informant, and I just observed the person that was wanted by authorities arrive, as well as the vehicle description, address, and apartment number. A short time later, a couple of county patrol vehicles showed up and went to the apartment. They were in there a few minutes and then exited with him in handcuffs.

Darla too was beneficial, but just not as much as her jobs and going to college, made it difficult for her to do as much. One day she called and asked if the Attorney General was in town. I said I didn't know and why she asked? She then told me that several FBI agents had just eaten dinner in her restaurant and there was a document left behind that gave information about the then Attorney General's full travel arrangements as well as information about his protection detail. I told her to hang on to it, to which she replied that she had given it to her boss in case these agents returned. I then contacted an agent that I had worked with at the FBI in Springfield, Missouri and informed him of the phone call. He advised that the Attorney General was indeed in town, and he knew the team leader and would call her to find out if anyone lost their operations plan. A short time later, he called me and advised that they had found out who left the documents behind. I went to the restaurant and recovered the documents from Darla's supervisor and turned it over to the local FBI Office. He then told me to thank my informant and appreciated the fact that the informant contacted me and that I called him. A few days later, I received a letter for my file and a second letter of appreciation to be placed in my informant's file. I passed the information on to Darla, who was excited to have been given the letter of appreciation.

We kept working, but so did Serguei. Serguei was still involved in criminal activity, and we continued to get complaints about him. Some of them made their way to me since I was in Springfield where he lived and knew his background and some of them did not. Welcome to the government.

Here are just a few that had been received during this in-between period.

In January 2002, INS received a written letter from a person known only as Mark, Last Name Unknown, who provided a statement, and in this statement, outlining what he knew of Serguei, his history in Russia, his family and his criminal contacts.

In July 2002, INS received a call from Wilson Steps, the owner of the Branson Postal Express in Branson, Missouri. Steps stated that Choukline is managing the Goodnight Inn in Branson, Missouri and is the manager of a Hotel Management Corporation. Steps said Serguei has been receiving a lot of letters from the Social Security Administration for a lot of different people in his personal mailbox. Steps provided copies of the front of the envelopes identifying whom the envelopes were addressed to, and a copy of the application completed by Choukline for the mailbox.

Later information received from Steps identified another thirty individuals receiving letters from the Social Security Administration. On another date in July 2002 Steps provided another forty-five names of individuals that had received letters from the Social Security Administration.

On July 15, 2002, INS received an anonymous call from an unknown caller advising that there were about fifty aliens employed by The Hacienda, a John Q. Hammonds Company in Branson, Missouri. The caller stated that there were 23 Jamaicans, 10 Polish, and an unknown number of Russian, Hungarian and Middle Easterners. The caller stated that the foreign nationals were being employed primarily in the housekeeping department and that they are all subcontract employees, and the subcontractors were taking a portion of the pay of the foreign nationals. It was unknown if the subcontractor was Serguei Choukline at this time.

Wilson Steps called again later in the month of July and stated that Choukline was housing his employees at the Fireside Inn as well as the Goodnight Inn, in Branson, Missouri. Steps provided another six names of individuals that received letters from the Social Security Administration. Steps later provided another seven names of persons receiving letters from the Social Security Administration.

We are into 2003 and things continue to change in the world of INS. As of March of 2003, INS no longer exist. INS, United States Customs Service, United States Secret Service,

Border Patrol, Customs Inspections Service and INS Inspectors and Examiners along with about 20 other agencies have been merged into the now United States Department of Homeland Security, Immigration and Customs Enforcement and for us, Homeland Security Investigations (HSI).

Even though we are going through the growing pains of the merger into a new agency, Serguei's criminal path continues forward, and we continued to gather further information into his criminal activity.

On June 30, 2003, Christi, Last Name Unknown, who was employed at the Never Late Shuttle, Branson, Missouri, stated that she had brought four individuals from Branson, Missouri to the HSI Office, Springfield, Missouri. Christi provided the names and information relating to these individuals as the following:

Samir Begollari, a citizen of Albania, who entered the United States on 06/25/03 as a J-1 exchange visitor authorized to remain in the United States until 10/25/03. A J-1 is a cultural exchange visitor that must have a residency of at least 2 years and can live and work across the United States during the time they are visiting the United States. They must return to their country before obtaining another type of visa to reenter the United States.

Ervin Canga, a citizen of Albania, who entered the United States on 05/20/03 as a J-1 Exchange Visitor, authorized to remain in the United States until 09/20/03.

Tomasz Sternik, a citizen of Poland, who last entered the United States on 06/24/03 as a J-1 Exchange Visitor, authorized to remain in the United States until 10/24/03.

Rafal Danilos, a citizen of Poland, who last entered the United States on 06/17/03 authorized to remain in the United States until 10/17/02.

All four of these individuals stated they had used the travel agency of Alturist/CET Poland/Cetusa/74 on the internet to find out about coming to the United States.

They stated that they were told in Poland that they must go to Branson, Missouri and would be met by someone who would take care of them and help get them jobs and Social Security Cards.

They said that they were each required to pay the following:

$150.00 deposit on the hotel

$100.00 to care for them

$150.00 to find a job for them and

$ 15.00 per week for transportation to work.

They said that they were all currently staying at the Musicians Inn hotel in Branson, Missouri.

One-time Serguei told them they must find a house or pay for the hotel, and then he told them that they must stay at the Musicians Inn. Serguei told them that they would be paid by check, but it is unknown to them if it were a personal or payroll check or if he would take out any deductions. They stated that there are currently one hundred people employed by Serguei Choukline.

In June 2003, Francis Hito, a United States citizen brought Rafal Mlynski and Darius Mikolajczyk to the HSI Office in Springfield, Missouri to speak to agents. Both provided information that they were H2B nonimmigrants employees who wanted to complain about their employer, Midwest Hotel Management Corporation (MWHMC).

They said that they believed that they were unfairly treated because they had to wait for two weeks before obtaining employment. They said their boss, was only known to them as Serguei. Serguei would not tell them his last name. They were wanting to know if they could switch employers.

Both Mlynski and Mikolajczyk had contracts from Alliances Abroad, which recruited them for MWHMC and outlined their pay and benefits. They were to be paid $6.50 per hour and work 35 to 40 hours per week. The contract stated that they could pay $130.00 per month for a hotel and $15.00 per week for transportation if necessary. Their main complaint was that they had not yet obtained employment. The address of MWHMC was identified as 1316 West Hwy 76, Suite 150, Branson, Missouri.

In November 2003, I received an anonymous letter which not only identified the previous INS investigation but appeared to know about our current inquiries into Serguei's activities. The letter identified tax evasion, employment and hiring practices, Choukline's weapons collection, and stated that he [Choukline], carries weapons in his car all the time. The letter indicated that Choukline has connections at the Branson, Missouri Police Department through a couple of his employees.

The letter further said that Choukline has all his employees living in hotels. It further stated that Choukline has his office at the Dynamic 7 Motel, 3060 Green Mountain Drive, Room 301, Branson, Missouri. The writer of the letter stated that Choukline has all his data in his home or on two laptop computers. The letter also stated that Choukline is extremely mobile and could destroy evidence in a matter of 15 minutes or less and provided license plate numbers for Choukline's vehicles.

On an unknown date, Szymon Kaczmarek, a citizen of Poland who last entered the United States on 06/25/02 as a J-1 Exchange Visitor and was authorized to remain in the United States until 10/25/02, came to the HSI Office I Springfield, Missouri to complain about Serguei.

Kaczmarek stated that he resided at 333 Parkside Drive, Hollister, Missouri and stated that he arranged for his trip to the United States through Organized Youth Travel in Warsaw, Poland. He stated that in 2002 he paid $7,800.00 for the plane ticket, and $1,200.00 to the organization to pay all fees.

Kaczmarek stated that he attended an organization meeting in Poland and was told that he had to wait for a job offer before he could leave for the United States. After two months he received a job offer from MWHMC. He stated that he looked on the Internet but could not find the address in Branson. He stated that the job offer was open ended and not specific. He stated that he was to be paid $5.00 an hour plus uniforms. He stated that he could refuse the job, but it may take a long time to get another offer and stated that he felt that it was better to accept and agree to the contract. He stated that his IAP-66 designated a specific company that he was to work for.

Kascmarek stated that he came into Springfield, Missouri by bus from New York. He stated that he was picked up by a Russian female about 25 years of age and she took five of them off the bus. There were two from Poland, and three from Hungary, and she transported all of them to Branson, Missouri.

Kaczmarek stated that they went to the Goodnight Inn where Serguei's office was in one of the rooms and met Serguei. Serguei told them that they would be put in hotel rooms and wait for a job offer. Serguei told them that he had one hundred students or more working for him. It was about five days later that he gave them a contract to sign. Serguei told them that he would transport them to work for $45.00 per month no matter what and that they would pay $450.00 per month if they wanted to stay in the room alone. If they wanted to share a room with four plus people to a room, they would split the cost. Kaczmarek stated that it was about one and a half weeks before he got a job at The Hacienda as a banquet server.

Kaczmarek stated that Choukline had a contract with The Hacienda for $8.00 per hour. He stated that at the beginning he was paid $6.00 per hour and at the end he was paid $6.25 per hour. He stated that he was told if he wanted a second job, he could do that only if he found it himself. There would be no cost incurred, but if Serguei had to find it for him, there was a fee that would be deducted from his check, usually about $15.00.

He stated that he was paid by check and there were no deductions listed. However, Choukline purportedly took taxes and deducted the cost of lodging and transportation from his check, but they were not listed.

Kacsmarek stated that the organization in Poland told him that he is required to work for his company. He was told if he left Choukline's employ, Choukline was to report it to the organization in Poland right away, and that he would be out of status and wanted by authorities, and he would not be allowed to reenter the United States. (H2B Visa holders are only allowed to work for the company that applied for them. If they wanted to work for someone else, they cannot work for that company until a new visa is approved).

Kacsmarek stated that he has never received any threats from Choukline. He stated that he was angry with Serguei because he continued to take money from him. Serguei would not allow him to leave work unless he made arrangements for one of the other foreign nationals to take his place or they had to pay a fee of $250.00 to leave. Kacsmarek did state that Serguei treated the Russians better than the Poles.

HSI also received information from Gale Gaines, who was employed by the Missouri Department of Labor, Division of Employment Security pertaining to the applications that had been filed by Serguei for H2B visas for employees. Gaines advised that she had been in contact with Richard Kline with the Department of Labor for the State of Missouri as well as the United States Department of Labor. Gaines advised that their preliminary investigation led to allegations of tax fraud not only at the State level but on the federal level as well.

As you can see, upon the completion of our first investigation of Serguei Choukline in 2001 and based on the complaints that we have received to date, he has now entered into a new fraud scheme. This one involving H2B Visa Fraud.

I did not have a case open yet; I was still in the intelligence gather phase of new leads. We were a new agency; I didn't want to make the same mistakes we made in the past. I wanted to make sure I presented a good case to be opened. I wanted to take advantage of any new tools available in my new toolbox. All of our management was beginning to change, case number, computer systems, programs, the whole nine yards. Some of the INS agents retired because they didn't want to be a part of the new agency. They were making comments derogatory to the Customs Service because of having to use their systems, saying this was a hostile takeover by Customs. Customs Agents didn't want to be associated with legacy INS agents either. No one like the name ICE, Customs comment was ICE stands for "Immigration Controls Everything." It was all a bunch of hooey as far as I was concerned. I was looking forward to the change, the combination of laws, training from the other agency, on both sides. This did nothing but enhance our authority and powers to better prosecute the bad guy and Serguei was the bad guy, and we are moving into the next phase of our investigation and hopefully be better able to enhance our investigation to the point of prosecution and conviction.

Informants are also an important tool in any law enforcement officers tool bag whether that officer is a federal, state, or local law enforcement officer and that was the same for me in our pursuit of Serguei Choukline. Due to Serguei's threats to his employees, people we contacted did not want to work with us for fear of retribution from Serguei. My informants didn't stop working though, they continued to be on the watch for any information about Serguei and his criminal activity. They weren't as afraid of him as others. Michael had been forced to serve in the Russian military as a young man and was no slouch himself. He was not afraid of Serguei and he himself had a falling out with Serguei at one time. It got so bad that they almost came to fisticuffs, but that did not happen. They parted ways, but the threats were still there. Serguei and a couple of his bullies if you will, Aleksandr Patsyukov and Victor Zhukovski were telling all of his other employees to stay away from Michael and Darla. He was telling them that Michael and Darla were the people that had been turning in all of the other employees that had been arrested by INS, which is what Serguei continued to call us. He told the other employees that Michael and Darla were informants for INS. Little did he know! Or did he? We will never know for sure.

Chapter Four

Investigation Two - A New Beginning

It was about mid-2004, and I was sitting in my temporary office in the now Springfield DHS/HSI Office, working on some paperwork when I had a visit from Special Agent John Cress, of the United States Department of Labor (DOL). Special Agent Cress was based out of Kansas City, Missouri, but he has had a long law enforcement career himself with the United States Secret Service during the Bill Clinton Presidency and before that with the Kansas City, Missouri Police Department. John was not new to criminal investigations, and I couldn't have worked this case with a better partner. As an investigator with the Department of Labor, part of his duty was to ensure that jobs in the United States were filled with persons who can legally fill those available jobs and if at all possible, with employees who are qualified to fill those positions. If people applying for those vacancies are foreign nationals, he too has to make sure the applications being filed through programs such as the H2B visa program and the J-1 Exchange Visitor programs are legitimate.

We went through our normal introductions, and I asked, "How can I help you?" John then told me that he had went to the HSI Office in Kansas City, Missouri and informed them that he was in the beginning stages of an investigation of Serguei Choukline who appears to be involved in H2B Visa Fraud. An H2B visa is a "Nonagricultural temporary Worker performing services unavailable in the United States". In other words, if a company needs employees to fill nonagricultural type jobs in the United States and have advertised for a period in the State that they are in, and cannot fill the positions, they can invite foreign nationals to fill the positions but only for a temporary period of time, usually during a peak season of tourist activity, which is only about 6 months or less, and they must return to their country.

There is a process for filing for these visas and that process is as follows.

- First the Petitioner (the person making the applications), submits temporary labor certification application to DOL. Before requesting H-2B classification from USCIS, the petitioner must apply for and receive a temporary labor certification for H-2B workers with the U.S. Department of Labor.

- Secondly. The Petitioner submits Form I-129 to USCIS. After receiving a temporary labor certification for H-2B employment from DOL, the petitioner must file Form I-129 with USCIS. With limited exceptions, the petitioner must submit the original temporary labor certification with Form I-129. If the application for a temporary labor certification was processed in DOL's FLAG system, the petitioner must include a printed copy of the electronic one-page "final determination" of the H-2B temporary labor certification approval with Form I-129.

USCIS will consider a printed copy of the final determination as the original and approved temporary labor certification. If a petitioner has already submitted the original temporary labor certification with a previous Form I-129, submit a copy of the temporary labor certification and provide an explanation that includes the receipt number of the petition with which the original was filed, if available.

- Thirdly, the prospective workers outside the United States apply for visa and/or admission. After USCIS approved Form I-129, the prospective H-2B workers who are outside the United States must:

- Apply for an H-2B visa with the U.S. Department of State (DOS) at a U.S. Embassy or Consulate abroad and then seek admission to the United States with U.S. Customs and Border Protection (CBP) at a U.S. port of entry; or

- Directly seek admission to the United States in H-2B classification with CBP at a U.S. port of entry in cases where an H-2B visa is not required.

Applications for H2B Temporary Workers may be only one application but may request multiple positions on one application. In most instances in Serguei's applications that were filed, he had no average number of positions on any of the applications.

What Serguei was doing, in a nutshell, was applying for H2B visas to fill vacant positions in the hotel/motel industry in and around the Branson, Missouri area. Positions he was attempting to fill were, housekeepers, banquet servers, waiters and waitresses and any other position identified as a temporary position needing to be filled during Branson's peak season.

It doesn't say it in the above requirements, but the reason why the State of Missouri Department of Labor became involved in the investigation is, because of the State's requirement for foreign workers to work in the state of Missouri. The job to be filled must be advertised for a period of time to show that the positions applied for cannot be filled by local workers.

John further identified that he too had received information from Gale Gaines with the Missouri Department of Labor; Division of Employment Security that Serguei's business is Midwest Hotel Management Corporation (hereafter MWHMC). It is also through the Division of Employment Security, that the applications are filed to show that a business has advertised for the appropriate amount of time. Again, this has to be done before filing for the use of foreign labor in the position that is being applied for. Based on the applications being filed with the State of Missouri, it was determined by them that Serguei, was using several other people to help him apply for the H2B visas and has applied for as many as three hundred foreign nationals from Russia, Poland, Armenia, Kazakhstan, and other countries by filing what she [Gale] believed to be false and fraudulent visa applications. Serguei created several fictitious business addresses, one of which was identified as 1316 West Highway 76, Suite 150, Branson, Missouri. This address was determined to be the Branson Postal Express and Suite #150 which was identified as an office was actually the Post Office Box number.

John further advised that he had found out through Gale Gaines, that Serguei had incorporated MWHMC as a business in about May of 2002 and was incorporated in the State of Missouri as a business that provides temporary foreign labor to the service industry, predominantly in and around Branson and Springfield, Missouri. These services included housekeeping personnel, restaurant staff, and various other aspects of the service industry that he provided foreign workers to. This information supports what INS/HSI had received from informers over the last couple of years.

John said it appeared that from about October of 2002 until now, MWHMC had filed a number of applications/petitions containing numerous false statements by the United States Mail, to the United States Bureau of Citizenship and Immigration Services in Lincoln, NE, US DOL, and the Department of Labor for the State of Missouri for several hundred foreign labor visas.

I informed John of the information that we had received between late 2001 and 2003, after the end of my first investigation of Serguei. I told him the INS and Homeland Security Investigation (HSI), had been receiving complaints about Serguei Choukline and Elena Moshennika identifying both their past and present criminal activity. In those complaints, we also determined that Serguei was using J-1 Exchange Visitors to fill his vacant positions in the hotel/motel industry in Branson and Springfield, Missouri.

There are certain procedures for a J-1 Exchange Visitor to enter the United States and those procedures are identified below.

- The J-1 classification (exchange visitors) is authorized for those who intend to participate in an approved program for the purpose of teaching, instructing, or lecturing, studying, observing, conducting research, consulting, demonstrating special skills, receiving training, or to receive graduate medical education or training.

- In carrying out the responsibilities of the Exchange Visitor Program, the Department of State designates public and private entities to act as exchange sponsors for J-1 nonimmigrants. These programs are designed to promote the interchange of persons, knowledge, and skills, in the fields of education, arts, and science.

Examples of exchange visitors include, but are not limited to:

Professors or scholars

Research assistants

Students

Trainees

Teachers

Specialists

Au Pairs

Camp counselors

- The U.S. Department of State plays the primary role in administering the J-1 exchange visitor program, so the first step in obtaining a J-1 visa is to submit a Form DS-2019,

Certificate of Eligibility for Exchange Visitor Status, (formerly known as an IAP-66). The sponsoring agency will provide this form. Applicants should work closely with the officials at the sponsoring agency who will be assisting the applicant through this process. An official who is authorized to issue Form DS-2019 is known as a responsible officer (RO) or alternate responsible officer (ARO).

- After a person has obtained a Form DS-2019, they may then apply for a J-1 visa through the U.S. Department of State at a U.S. Embassy or Consulate. The waiting time for an interview appointment for applicants can vary, so submitting a visa application as early as possible is strongly encouraged (though applicant may not enter the United States in J-1 status more than 30 days before their program begins).

John and I discussed Serguei and Elena's previous criminal investigation and how it ended. We discussed the cooperation with the State of Missouri Department of Labor and their Division of Employment Security. Since I had ten volumes of investigation into Serguei's past, I had a lot of information about his history, his background, his family, his contacts at local police departments and how he developed those contacts, news articles of Serguei's involvement in the community as it relates to student exchange programs, getting his name in the paper with the Sheriff of a County or the Chief of Police of a particular city. How Serguei used the Post Office Drop Boxes to hide or cover his criminal activity.

As we looked through the books associated with the previous investigation and discussed the mistakes made by INS not on the part of the investigators, at least not that we are aware of, but I told him of the systemic and procedural flaws in the application review process at the Service Center, that partially caused the prosecution of the first investigation to be declined. I did not hold anything back, I told him about everything. I felt that he needed to know about all of it as we moved forward with this investigation.

One particular systemic flaw that I previously spoke to and that was maintaining the envelope that identified where the applications were mailed from and who mailed them. This was a big issue.

There were a couple of other issues as well, in that INS investigations had the local ADDI that oversaw investigations, but then there was the District Director (DD) that oversaw both Investigations and Examinations, what is now called Citizenship and Immigration Services. The ADDI had to brief him on large scale investigations, and he was also the person who the ADDI had to go through for additional funding for large-scale investigations. Our DD had previously been in the Border Patrol and Inspections but had never been a criminal investigator. He had been away from the law enforcement aspects of things within the agency for a while and was focused more on Examinations or what we called "The giveaway program," the side of Immigration that approved or denied benefits.

This program was self-funded; therefore, all of the funds that were brought into this program by foreign nationals applying for a benefit went back into the program. By the money coming back into the program, it allowed them to fill vacant positions, buy furniture or office supplies with these funds. Needless to say, it was difficult to get an examiner to deny a benefit. At times it was like pulling teeth even though the evidence was there, many times they just ignored it and approved a benefit anyway. In Kansas City, the amount of time that was allowed for an interview was about 15 minutes. If it went over 15 minutes, I've seen supervisors call the examiner and want to know what was taking so long. If the examiner requested a denial, he/she had to document the case to the hilt (which should be the case no matter what) before it was denied and sometimes it still didn't get denied. There was a quota on the number of citizenships that were granted for the month or the quarter. There was a glass case mounted on the wall at the end of the hallway leading into the Examination Section with their goal and a running total of the benefits approved. It was a crazy setup and made it difficult at times for us as criminal investigators to get foreign nationals who have committed fraud to be denied a benefit and put into removal proceedings.

  John and I discussed all of these things; I would guess over the rest of the day. We were trying to determine the best way to move forward on our investigation, who to ask for assistance, if anyone else at this time. (I had told him about the issue with the FBI at the end of the first investigation). We had to decide when to present to or if we had enough to present to a United States Attorney and then where? Should it be presented in Springfield, Missouri because it was local to where Serguei lived and where he was conducting most of his criminal activity, or Kansas City, Missouri, to the same Organized Crime Strike Force who looked at the first investigation and who subsequently denied it. It was originally taken to Kansas City, Missouri because of Serguei's own claims of being involved in Organized Crime, they had already looked at it once and they too knew his background and how manipulative and elusive he could be and how he treated his employees. It was not much of a discussion at this point, it was decided it would be referred to Kansas City, Missouri United States Attorney's Office Organized Crime Strike Force for prosecution assistance in this Investigation as well.

Why do we need to go to the United States attorney's office for assistance? Without the assistance or oversight of the United States Attorney Office, there is no way to present the case for prosecution. A grand jury is put into place to hear your evidence and agree or disagree to proceed with charges, so a case has to go to a grand jury, the grand jury will also approve the issuance of a grand jury subpoenas for information which is supposed to be confidential until trial. The Assistant United States Attorney is the person we go through to obtain search warrants for people, emails, and business records, as well as seizure warrants for vehicles, homes, and businesses. There has to be approval from a United States Attorney for many aspects of an investigation. Without those approvals, the case goes nowhere. It doesn't ever get to the judge.

It was determined that we would go back to our respective agencies and gather whatever information there was to determine Serguei's continued involvement in criminal activity and would get together at a later date.

John would also go back to the Missouri Department of Labor, Division of Employment Security and gather copies of all the applications and evidence submitted in support of those applications to determine if a criminal investigation at the federal level was truly warranted.

We said our goodbyes and began our respective background investigations.

John did just what we discussed and went to his agency and the Missouri Department of Labor and contacted Gale Gaines with the Division of Employment Security and obtained copies of all of their records and application and evidence submitted in support of those applications.

I then went to what is now known as Citizenship and Immigration Services and obtained the applications/petitions for H2B Visas and the evidence/documents submitted in support of the applications/petitions. This was done internally, within our own respective agencies, so there was no requirement for warrants or subpoenas.

Again, I can't reiterate enough, that upon completion of our first investigation of Serguei Choukline in 2001 for L1A Intracompany Transferee Visa Fraud, he immediately began this new criminal scheme involving H2B Non-Agricultural Worker and J-1 Exchange Visitor Visa Fraud. It is all he knows how to do, it seemed like it was in his blood.

All of this intelligence gathering was not conducted overnight. It took time, probably at least three months, for John to get the applications that had been filed from the State of Missouri and from the United States Department of Labor, as well as for me to get the applications that had been processed through INS and now Citizenship and Immigration Services.

We also had to locate and collect the reports of interview of the people that had contacted both legacy INS and now HSI. Then once we received all of the documents through our respective agency's procedures, we had to sit down and revue them, compare them to each other to make sure we are correct in our summary of what was going on in the criminal visa fraud scheme.

In the beginning of September 2004, we felt that we had enough to go to the United States Attorney and present our case for consideration for oversight of the investigation. We called AUSA Paul Becker, the supervisor of the Organized Crime Strike Force, Kansas City, Missouri, and briefed him quickly on the telephone advising him that we are once again looking at Serguei Choukline, this time for H2B Visa Fraud and J-1 Exchange Visitor Fraud. He agreed that it needed to be discussed and looked at again and a meeting was set up.

On September 23, 2004, our meeting was held in Kansas City, Missouri with Assistant United States Attorney, Paul Becker, Supervisor, Organized Crime Strike Force Unit, Western District of Missouri, and a couple of his attorneys, AUSA David Barnes, and AUSA Bruce Clark (who was the attorney on the first investigation of Serguei, the one who declined to proceed further). Even though the investigation was in Springfield and Branson, Missouri area, about two hundred miles south of Kansas City, Missouri, the Organized Crime Strike Force for the Western District of Missouri covered all of Western Missouri, which includes the Branson and Springfield, Missouri area. Others present for the meeting besides me, with HSI, and John Cress, Special Agent, United States Department of Labor, there was a Special Agent with the Internal Revenue Service, and Richard Kline, Investigator, Missouri Department of Labor. This meeting was held to present an up-to-date overview of our new investigation of Serguei to the United States Attorney's Office for consideration for oversight and prosecution.

The meeting revealed that Serguei D. Choukline has claimed both an income and a loss of as much as 1.8 million dollars through his companies, both MWHMC his legitimate company and AAA Hotel Services Inc, a newer company. Both are reportedly owned by Serguei Choukline. In review of these businesses by the State of Missouri and the IRS there is no indication that appropriate taxes and deductions are being taken from the payroll of Serguei's foreign-born employees, nor is he paying the prevailing wage as required by law under the program.

What is a prevailing wage? This should be defined before we go any further and this is the best definition, I could find on open-source information which is as follows:

- Prevailing wages are rates for wages and fringe benefits set by the Department of Labor (DOL) that employers with government contracts or foreign workers must pay their employees. The prevailing wage rates vary by location and are based on the average wages employees with similar roles receive in the area. Employers who take on federal contracts must pay the rate. Many states also have laws requiring employers who take on state contracts to pay the prevailing wage rate.

The information provided by The United States Department of Labor and the Missouri Department of Labor along with Homeland Security, it was determined that there is a large discrepancy regarding the number of employees that he has reported over the last several years to the Department of Labor for the State of Missouri. Agents of the Department of Labor and HSI, have conducted several interviews (the previously received complaints and interviews conducted in person and telephonic between 2001 and 2003), and have received the same types of reports and determined through our own reviews of the applications there have been several false and fraudulent statements made on the applications and petitions filed with the respective agencies.

Based on the evidence and interviews, it appears that several violations of federal law have possibly been perpetrated to include the following.

- Title 8, USC, Section 1324, in that Serguei Choukline, has falsified or made false statements in the ETA-750 form filed with the Department of Labor in an attempt to obtain a large number of H2B visas which will be used to obtain employees for his service-oriented business of supplying housekeeping personnel to the hotel/motel industry in and around Branson, Missouri.

- Title 18, USC, Section 1341, Mail Fraud, in that Serguei Choukline has used or caused to be used, the United States Postal System to mail the fraudulent and falsified ETA-750's to the State of Missouri the United States Department of Labor and the Bureau of Citizenship and Immigration Services to obtain visas for person he has induced to come to and work in the United States for his service-oriented business.

- Title 18, USC, Section 1546, Visa Fraud, in that Serguei Choukline, by falsifying the ETA-750, to the State of Missouri, Department of Labor and the Bureau of Citizenship and Immigration Services, had obtained the H2B visas by fraud and false statements to all agencies involved. Serguei Choukline has also made arrangements with travel agencies in various countries to obtain J-1 Exchange Visitors, which are brought to the United States for a period of four months to work specifically for his business, MWHMC, and other fictitious businesses reportedly owned by him or his co-conspirators to supply housekeeping personnel to the hotel/motel industry in and around Branson, Missouri, and the surrounding area.

- Title 18, USC, 1581(a) and 1584, Involuntary Servitude and Peonage, in that Serguei Choukline, along with his co-conspirators knowingly used the H2B Temporary Worker visa and the J-1 Visitor Exchange Visa fraud scam to induce and lure citizens of foreign countries to come to and remain in the United States and work for Serguei Choukline's business to supply employees to the hotel/motel industry in and around Branson, Missouri. Serguei Choukline and his co-conspirators through the fraud scheme held the employees (victims) in involuntary servitude in that the employees were required to work for Serguei Choukline and his co-conspirators. If the employee wanted to leave, he has to find his own replacement, or pay a fee to Serguei Choukline. Serguei Choukline threatened the employee with being out of status and would be wanted and never be able to return to the United States. The employees were required to pay for transportation to and from work, rent for the hotel room, and they were required to resided in one hotel room with as many as three others who may or may not have been known to them at the time of their arrival in Branson, Missouri.

- Title 18, USC, Section 1956, Money Laundering, in that Serguei Choukline is using the proceeds from the employment of H2B Temporary Workers and J-1 Exchange Visitors, that he obtained through visa fraud and tax violations to purchase vehicles, to pay for his home, and further violations of the above specified unlawful activity as it relates to Title 8, USC, 1324. And

At the request of the United States Attorney, IRS will investigate the aspects of a tax evasion, which could take a few years. This would constitute a violation of Title 26, USC, Section 7201, Income Tax Evasion, in that Serguei Choukline failed to properly file Federal Income Taxes. Several Grand Jury subpoenas will be requested for bank records to look at once the structuring habits of Choukline have been identified. The Assistant United States Attorney accepted the investigation and AUSA's David Barnes, and Bruce Clark were assigned from their office. Since INS/HSI has had a previous investigation into Serguei Choukline and have an in-depth background on him, HSI has been made the lead investigative agency with Department of Labor as second, but as far as I was concerned, we were co-equals! The new investigation officially begins!

Chapter Five

Midwest Hotel Management Corporation (MWHMC)

Who or what is Midwest Hotel Management Corporation or MWHMC as we will call it? We started getting information about this company at the end of the first investigation, but since Serguei had absconded back to Russia, and was facing charges there, it was at the time kind of a moot point! We thought he would go to jail for a long time, especially on a murder charge in Russia! Then we had the terrorist attack on September 11, 2001, and that put a stop to about everything proactive, everything was terrorist related, Joint Terrorism Task Forces, Liaison Officers to the FBI in smaller cities like Springfield, Missouri, lists of names of persons to be interviewed being sent to the field, and details to Washington D.C. After things calmed down, we were all starting to regroup, and we started to look at the investigations that had been put on the back burner because of the terrorist attacks on the United States.

The activity of MWHMC is one of those investigations. This company was initially brought to us by Gale Gaines, at the Missouri Department of Labor, Division of Employment Security. The information that was given, indicated that

MWHMC had submitted several fraudulent applications for H2B Temporary Worker Visas. As we said earlier, the H2B Temporary Worker Visa Program is designed to allow foreign workers to work in certain industries to provided labor after it has been determined that there is a legitimate need for the work and that there is an insufficient number of citizens or other legal aliens to provide the labor.

In about May of 2002, just a short time after INS completed its first investigation into the L1A Visa Fraud Scam, Serguei began a new scheme. MWHMC was incorporated in the States of Missouri as a business that provides temporary foreign labor to the service industry. MWHMC has predominantly provided this service in and around the Branson and Springfield, Missouri area. The services, as we have continued to say include providing, housekeeping personnel, restaurant staff and various other aspects of the service industry requesting businesses.

From about October 2002 until now, MWHMC had submitted fifteen applications/petitions containing numerous false statements, by the United States mail to the United States Bureau of Citizenship and Immigration Services in Lincoln, NE for about two hundred and fifty foreign labor visas. We know through our research in preparation to present this investigation to the United States Attorney's Office, that Serguei, through MWHMC had filed these fifteen separate visa applications with the various agencies that are involved in this investigation. Legacy INS, United States Department of Labor, and the Missouri Department of Labor, Division of Employment Security.

As we researched for these applications in September 2004, we found that in 2003, there were five visa applications filed; one was for a person named Irina Lemetyuynen for L1A Intracompany Transferee, and four others for H2B Temporary Worker visas. One of these four visa applications was for eighty-nine workers, another for twenty-nine workers, another for twenty workers and another for ten workers, for a total of one hundred and forty-eight workers and counting Lemetyuynen for one hundred and forty-nine in 2003,

In 2004, there was another ten applications filed. There were at least four filed for individual people for the L1A Intracompany Transferee workers; there were two filed in the name of Agnieska Koblenc. There were two filed, because the first one was denied, but the second one was approved. There was another filed in the name of Patricia Ribiero for an L1A visa and a fourth for Monica Lopez-Rodriguez for an L1A. The rest of the visa applications, which is the additional six applications were filed for H2B Temporary Worker visas. The first for five, the next for only one, the next for four, another for thirteen. Then the numbers began to go up, as the next one was for twenty-eight and then the last was for forty-five, for a total number of H2B visas at ninety -six, plus the four L1A visa application and the total is now another one hundred for 2004. Therefore between 2003 and 2004, he has applied through MWHMC for a total of two hundred and forty-four visas purportedly for his business, and to fill vacant labor positions in and around Branson, and Springfield, Missouri. They were all signed by Anton Kim. Who the heck is this guy? Is this Serguei's boss or underling? We need to find him!

MWHMC is a pretty active business to be filing for the number of visas that have been applied for over just a two-year period. Who are the companies that need this many employees? How did they come to know about MWHMC or how to contact the company? We saw in our past complaints that many of the individuals that turned on Serguei or complained about him, spoke mostly about a person named Monica that helped him conduct his business. She was the one who was with Serguei a lot, she was the one that paid them their pay checks and she [Monica] was the go-to person if there was a human resources or personnel issue, or if there were any complaints about their work or housing or any other issues that may arise.

How did they get their employees to Branson and Springfield, Missouri? Was it as sporadic as was described to us by persons that were brought to the office to be interviewed, those who complained of mal treatment by Serguei, no pay or late paychecks? What was the business operation and since there are multiple addresses for the business, where did they function out of?

So, where is MWHMC? We know it operated in Branson, Missouri. In our investigation with the assistance of the Missouri Division of Employment Security, were able to determine one of the addresses he was using was that of 1316 W. Highway 76, Suite 150, Branson, Missouri. We also identified several other addresses associated with MWHMC. These other addresses were 3000 Green Mountain Drive, Branson, Missouri, 210 S. Wildwood Drive, Branson, Missouri and 305 East Walnut, Suite 110A, Springfield, Missouri.

John and I traveled to the initial address of 1316 West Highway 76, Suite 150 in Branson, Missouri because of information we had previously received from people who had called and provided information to us in the past. It was verified that this address was nothing more than a drop box, Branson Postal Express, the Suite 150 was his mailbox. We identified ourselves and spoke briefly to the person working behind the counter who informed us that this Post Office Box was used by MWHMC and, what is interesting is that it is also used by another company by the name of AAA Hotel Services. Both companies are receiving mail at this address, and both are owned or operated by Serguei Choukline.

Based on the complaints that we had received earlier identifying places where Serguei had his offices or housed the foreign nationals he employed, we went to the Goodnight Inn, 210 South Wildwood Drive, Branson, Missouri. This address was also used as the business office addresses for MWHMC. We met with the manager of the hotel, in the office behind the front counter. He was behind his desk and John and I across from him in a couple of straight back but somewhat comfortable chairs. The manager was cordial and cooperative in speaking to us as we conducted our interview. He was asked as everyone will be asked; Do you know Serguei Choukline, have you done business with MWHMC, does Serguei have an office here at this location, and do you use his workers. The managers said "Serguei supplied us employees for our housekeeping staff, but he has never received permission or authority to use this hotel or address as a business address."

The last address used by MWHMC in Branson, Missouri was identified as 3000 Green Mountain Drive, Branson, Missouri. This address turned out to be another drop box identified as We Box It! This address is another address used by AAA Hotel Services Inc. This is the other business identified as owned or operated by Serguei Choukline in his business of supplying employees to local businesses. There was no one present at this time that would be able to answer any of our questions.

We returned to Branson Postal Express, located at 1316 West Highway 76, Branson, Missouri before heading north to Springfield, Missouri, and this time interviewed Wilson Steps, the manager. Wilson reiterated what we were continuing to hear and that is, "Monica Lopez-Rodriguez, is the person that had been picking up the mail from mailbox 150 since about June or July of 2004". He added that "The Mailbox is registered to Serguei Choukline and the address for Serguei is on West Suzanne Place, Springfield, Missouri."

After we left the Branson Postal Express, John and I proceeded north to the last address that we were aware of at the time. This address, 305 East Walnut, Suite 110A, Springfield, Missouri. For those of you who do not know the Ozarks, Branson, Missouri is just forty miles south of Springfield, Missouri on Highway 65. Highway 76 is the main highway that goes through the center of Branson and is where most of the shows and sightseeing occurs. Branson has expanded quite a bit over the years and there are many more highways and roadways through the city. If you have heard of Silver Dollar City, or have ever been there, it is a theme park on the west side of Branson, Missouri on Highway 76.

As John and I checked out the address in Springfield, Missouri, we were able to interview Gina Sharp, the Rental Manager for the Vandecort Building, 305 East Walnut, Suite 110A, Springfield, Missouri. Sharp told us that "Serguei Choukline rented the address from November 2002 until August 2004." Sharp added that "The suite was usually unoccupied, but periodically would see Serguei Choukline and his wife Irina Choukline and an unidentified white female."

Who was this other white female along with Serguei's wife at the business address of MWHMC in Springfield, Missouri? Was that Agnieska Koblenc who had been filed for in 2003 or Monica who was filed for in 2004, who is a Hispanic. Maybe whoever saw this white female was actually seeing a Hispanic female? Who knows, and these are answers that we need to find out, to better understand the business of MWHMC. How they functioned, how they operated?

We identified through the list of visas that Serguei had filed in 2004 the visa for Monica Lopez-Rodriguez. We recovered the application/petition filed on her behalf and began to look at it more closely. As we looked at the Form I-129, a Petition for Nonimmigrant Worker as an L1A Intracompany Transferee, that was filed on behalf of Monica Lopez-Rodriguez, also known as (AKA); Monica Alejandra Lopez-Rodriguez; AKA: Monica A. Lopez; AKA: Monica Volkov and AKA: Monica A. Volkov filed on July 28, 2004, we found that it was filed just three months before our investigation began. We also found that it was for the position of the Director of Human Resources for MWHMC.

The application for Monica Lopez-Rodriguez stated that she had been employed by the parent or holding company of MWHMC, identified as TOO Sovtek, located in Vavilova, Moscow, Russia from 2002 until 2004 with no interruption in employment. What was interesting about Monica is that she is from Mexico but is purported to have worked for the TOO SOVTEC, the parent company of MWHMC in Russia. Why was a Mexican female working for two years in Russia? Why did she go to Russia? How did she get there? Questions we will certainly ask her at a later date. I feel it is important to always remember, the first investigation into Serguei's criminal activity was for what. L1A, Intracompany Transferee Visa Fraud. Serguei is awfully familiar with the procedures for filing for this type of visa. The application for Monica was subsequently approved on August 12, 2004.

Monica Lopez-Rodriguez was now an L1A, Intra Company Transferee and is purported to be working, per the application, at the address of 1316 West Highway 76, Suite 150, Branson, Missouri, which if you remember is the address of the Branson Postal Express which housed the mailbox for MWHMC. John and I laughed and joked about her fitting into mailbox 150 and conducting her work from there.

On September 21, 2004, before our meeting on the 23rd in Kansas City, Missouri with the AUSA, we spoke with Steve Manson, the Hotel Manager and Sharon Mays, the Human Resources Manager at The Hacienda, Branson, Missouri. Both were asked if they had conducted business with MWHMC and Serguei Choukline. Both stated, "We have been doing business with MWHMC since 2002 and have employed approximately one hundred foreign laborers provided by Serguei." They went on to say, "During the time we used his employees, we communicated by use of emails (which we will identify later), and Serguei and Monica Lopez are our points of contact for MWHMC." Monica, Monica, Monica is what we continued to hear and will continue to hear is the "Point of Contact" for the employees and the businesses as it relates to MWHMC. Monica has now become one of our main targets of this investigation. We needed to focus a large amount of our attention on Monica Lopez-Rodriguez and as she seemed to be the face of MWHMC and was fully aware of how it operated.

Michael on November 19, 2004, called me and informed me that he had met a person by the name of Denis Butuzov, who told Michael that he worked for Serguei Choukline at MWHMC and that he [Denis], had a serious drinking problem to the point of alcoholism. Denis told the informant that he was late for work several times because of hangovers and Serguei called an all employees meeting at one of the hotels where he kept his employees (Denis did not tell which hotel). Serguei commenced to make an example of him in front of the other employees and Serguei physically beat Denis pretty badly in front of the other employees and told them "If you screw with me this is what will happen. I have friends with INS and with the Police and I will have you arrested, deported, and sent back to your country!" This is the initial story that was told to Michael by Denis as to what happened to him.

Michael stated that he has tried to find Denis again but couldn't find him. I told him we needed to find Denis so I could speak to him about Serguei's business and how he was treated.

We, though still trying to find out who Anton Kim is, are also trying to find Denis Butuzov.

Just a short time later, probably within a couple of weeks, Michael called and said that he had heard from others in the Russian community that Denis was in Little Rock, Arkansas working at the Peterson Hotel. So, I sent a collateral request for the agents in Little Rock to attempt to locate him, and they did!

On December 16, 2004, Special Agents in Little Rock, Arkansas had found and apprehended Denis Butuzov at his residence in Little Rock. He was arrested for being an out of status J-1 Exchange Visitor. Agents of Little Rock, agreed to meet me and another agent from Springfield, Missouri in Marshall, Arkansas where we took custody of Denis and transported him to the Springfield HSI Office. We made the meet, took Denis back to Springfield, and put him in the local jail where we house our prisoners.

On December 17, 2004, I interviewed Denis in regard to his employment with MWHMC. Denis told me that he entered the United States on May 29, 2002, at New York City, New York as a J-1 Exchange Visitor. He said that he initially travelled to Memphis, Tennessee to visit a friend by the name of Alex Gloukov. He said that Gloukov is the person that told him about Serguei in Branson. Evidently Gloukov and Serguei used to be friends and he was told by Gloukov that he could go to work for Serguei. Denis said that Gloukov is the one who brought him to Springfield to work for Serguei. Denis said that he was to be paid a certain amount of money and was told directly by Serguei that he did not need to worry about taxes. He said that he was required to sign a contract with Serguei and began working for him in about July of 2002.

Denis said that he had been out at a nightclub and had walked back to his hotel. When he arrived at the hotel at about 5:00 AM, Serguei came out of the hotel, walked up to him and with a closed fist knocked him to the ground. Serguei did this in front of about 15 other employees. He was directed by Serguei to leave and not to come back.

Denis said that he had only heard about the threats of Serguei's to his employees until his own encounter with him. He said that he had heard the threats of calling immigration and having them, the employees, deported if they failed to follow Serguei's instructions. He said that Serguei ran his company like a military operation. Serguei would tell everyone that he could have them sent to jail due to his relationship with the law enforcement community. Serguei did his best to keep his employees on a short leash.

Denis went on to say that Serguei bragged about killing a man in Russia and getting away with it. Serguei told him directly that the person he killed was a weak person and should have died. Denis said that he believed that Serguei was a dangerous man based on his discussion about killing a man and his own encounter with him

Denis returned for a second interview on December 28, 2004, a couple of weeks later. He stated that he needed to correct his original statement stating that he misled agents because he was afraid of Serguei. Denis went on to say that the only difference is what he told us about how it all took place. He said that he had been out drinking with a person named Igor Broytman, a resident alien in the United States, and two female Russian students in Hollister, Missouri. He said that the others left, and he was given the keys to Igor's vehicle. He said that he wasn't going to sit and wait, so he took the car and left. He went driving around, got lost and couldn't find his way back so he went back to his hotel.

Denis told me that that part about Serguei coming out of the hotel and hitting him in front of other employees was all true. Serguei got into a green Ford Expedition and left to go pickup Igor. He said that he stayed there for another four or five days staying in the rooms of friends and then he departed.

Denis was asked if he was willing to work with me as an informant and provide information about Serguei and MWHMC. Denis admitted that he had a drinking problem and that he was indeed afraid of Serguei. Denis went on to say that if he heard of anyone that was willing to turn in Serguei and wanted to complain about him, he would have them call me. I gave him a business card should he encounter someone that wanted to talk to me so he could give them my telephone number. Denis was placed in removal proceedings and was subsequently released on bond.

In early April of 2005, because of our inability to locate the true MWHMC operating location, we contacted HSI Asset Removal Group in Chicago, IL our then Office of the Special Agent in Charge or SAC Office for assistance in identifying all of Serguei Choukline's assets here in the United States. This group is amazing and has the tools if you will, to locate and identify property owned and operated by a person or business. The request was made, and they went to work.

We are still trying to identify, the main guy of MWHMC with the name of Anton Kim. We have all searched his name in all of our accessible data bases and still cannot find an Anton Kim not only not associated with MWHMC, but we can't even find Anton Kim residing in the United States or if anyone with this name has ever traveled to or departed from the United States.

We were contacted by Gayle Gaines from the Missouri Division of Employment Security who informed John and I that she had received several emails from a person known as "Anton Kim" using the email address midwestcorp@yahoo.com. John and I discussed this information with AUSA David Barnes, who was the primary AUSA assigned to this case. AUSA Barnes authorized an undercover operation at the State of Missouri Division of Employment Security, if the State concurred to allow Gayle to conduct one on one training with the MWHMC staff to include Anton Kim and Serguei Choukline. This was to be done in an attempt to determine if Anton Kim and Serguei Choukline were one in the same. The Department of Labor, Division of Employment Security authorized Gayle to conduct the undercover operation so I began through our undercover guys to setup and make arrangements for a day of training in Jefferson City, Missouri, the day the employees of MWHMC would come to participate.

In late April of 2005, the training room with the authorization of the State of Missouri Division of Employment

Security and with Gayle's cooperation, was wired with video and audio for the operation. The training for Anton Kim and Serguei Choukline of MWHMC who were to arrive and attend one on one training on "How to Apply for H2B Visas to Fill Vacant Positions in the State of Missouri with Foreign Born Nationals." The training was going to take place between one and four o'clock on a particular date. The training was going to be monitored by agents from an adjoining room. However, I believe it to be Monica who called and stated that Anton Kim had to leave town on an urgent matter and would not be available to attend the training and it was cancelled. So now, we are back to the drawing board in our attempt to determine if Serguei Choukline and Anton Kim are indeed one in the same person.

In early 2005, we found that my wife's father in Kansas City had been diagnosed with prostate cancer. We still lived in the Springfield, Missouri area and my wife began traveling back and forth the six-to-seven-hour round trip to go with him to doctors' appointments and to just help where she could. My wife's sister worked a full-time job, and it was more difficult for her to take off work to go with him to each of his appointments so my wife decided that she would help where she could. If it came to a point where she couldn't make the trip for some reason, her sister would absolutely take off.

On one particular trip in early 2005, it was still considered late winter 2004, my wife as usual by herself had travelled to Kansas City to help her dad. She was on her way back home, it was getting late, and a fluke snow storm came up. We had cell phones by that time, and she called me and told me of the weather conditions where she was on southbound 71 Highway, now Interstate 49 was not good, and she was having a difficult time seeing the highway. The snow was really starting to come down and she was still a couple of hours away from home. We discussed it and decided it would be safer for her to get a hotel room in Harrisonville, Missouri. So, here she is without all of the amenities that a woman would usually take with her on a trip and having to get a hotel room by herself.

We have always tried to be safety conscious and not really a big fan of her staying by herself at a hotel room two hours from home. She made do, the hotel usually always has shampoo and soap and things like that in the room, and now a days, they even have hair driers in the room as well. She was able to get by for one night, got up early and headed home. Thank the Lord the roads had been kept pretty clear overnight and she made it home safely.

So, after this little incident, I began the process of trying to get back to the Kansas City office. In July, one of the agents in Kansas City, left for a position in Arkansas and the Assistant Special Agent in Charge, contacted my Resident Agent in Charge, as he is now called, in Springfield and told him that if I was still interested in coming to Kansas City, and was willing to pay for my own transfer, to submit the paperwork through channels and he would push it up to Chicago. Since the transfer was a transfer request within our own SAC area, I guess the SAC in Chicago could approve the transfer. So, I did just that and in August of 2005 I transferred back to the Kansas City office of the Assistant Special Agent in Charge. It was certainly a blessing with the concerns of my wife's dad.

Since the investigation was being handled by the Organized Crime Strike Force Unit with the Office of the United States Attorney in Kansas City, Missouri, the investigation of Serguei Choukline remained my investigation. So, it made my contacts with John and the AUSA much easier. Usually when you transfer from one office to another, all of your investigations are transferred to another agent, and you start afresh in the new office. In this case, I kept the investigation. I did pick up some local small cases since I was now going to be traveling from Kansas City to the Branson and Springfield, Missouri area quite frequently. It took me a couple of weeks to get moved into our new home, but it all worked out and now it was time to get back to work.

Continuing our investigation into MWHMC and the hotels and motels that they supplied employees to in the Branson, Missouri area we determined that we should start looking at Monica and Serguei's addresses to determine where the business operation was being conducted.

However, through my first investigation, I attempted to surveil Serguei's home address on West Suzanne Place in Springfield, Missouri. This address is on the south side of Springfield, Missouri and was on a Cul-de-Sac and his residence was at the end. It was exceedingly difficult to watch. We couldn't set down the street because of the neighborhood watch committee, they will definitely call the police. You don't want to have to explain to local law enforcement why you are sitting there watching a house, because then the neighbors wonder why you weren't forced to leave, and if the target of your surveillance is watching, you have brought attention to yourself.

We were unable to surveil Serguei's residence in that case and in this investigation as well.

Still trying to determine the true location of MWHMC operating location, we started looking at the most likely person that could lead us to it and that is Monica Lopez-Rodriguez and who knows if there is an Anton Kim, maybe he will show up, or she will go meet him somewhere. We can only hope! On September 21, 2005, John and I began to conduct surveillance of 111 Crosby Street, Branson, Missouri, the residence of Monica Lopez-Rodriguez. This address had been obtained from her Missouri driver license. The home was located on a dead-end street as well, but the surrounding area allowed for a place to sit and watch without drawing attention to ourselves, unlike that of Serguei's residence. There was only one vehicle seen at the residence which was a dark green Ford Minivan, Missouri license 737-TXM, which was registered to MWHMC. 1316 W. Highway 76, Branson, Missouri. We have at least verified where she lives.

In October 2005, John and I again made contact with Sharon Mays, the Director of Human Resources for The Hacienda Resort, Branson, Missouri, who is assisting in our investigation. Susan agreed to conduct a consensually monitored telephone call to a telephone number which had been provided to her by Monica Lopez-Rodriguez. Sharon made the call and asked for Monica who had answered the telephone. Sharon told Monica "I needed to speak to Anton Kim pertaining to next year's foreign labor issues." Monica Lopez-Rodriguez told Sharon that "Anton rarely comes to Missouri and spends most of his time in New York or Florida. The point of contact in Missouri is Serguei." The fact that Anton Kim rarely comes to Missouri is an important fact as this investigation moves forward.

In November of 2005, during another week-long trip to Branson, Missouri, John, and I interviewed Nathan and John, the owners of Cotton Enterprises Inc. Both looking back and forth at each other, said "We have been doing business with MWHMC since 2003 and have employed about sixty of his workers." "During this time MWHMC communicated with us by way of emails and faxes." "MWHMC provided us a contact telephone number and told us that he [Serguei Choukline] and Monica Lopez-Rodriguez were our points of contact."

On November 15, 2005, John and I again conducted surveillance of 111 Crosby Street, Branson, Missouri, the residence of Monica Lopez-Rodriguez. We sat and watched the residence I am guessing for a couple of hours both the last time and this time and there was no activity. There was only one vehicle seen at the residence which was the same vehicle seen on our previous surveillance, and that vehicle was a dark green Ford Minivan, Missouri license 737-TXM, which was registered to MWHMC. 1316 W. Highway 76, Branson, Missouri.

In November 2005, John, and I this time met with Jeffrey Patterson, the owner of Goodnight Inn where Serguei housed his employees and claimed to have an office at that location or led others to believe that he had a business office located at this address. I remember it being a slow day at the hotel, no one else being around, so John and I stood across from him at the front counter as we discussed their use of MWHMC and what he knew about Serguei, listening, and making our notes.

Jeffrey said "Serguei Choukline is the person I believed to be the owner of MWHMC." Jeffrey went on to say "Serguei stayed at the Goodnight Inn and housed several of his employees at the hotel in exchange for services as housekeepers and front desk staff." Jeffrey said "Serguei had asked him if he could use his storage closet as an office for his company. He said he told him he could not as there is not heat or air conditioning in the storage room nor is there a telephone and the space is being used for storage for the hotel." Jeffrey stated, "At no time did I ever give Serguei permission to use the address of Goodnight Inn in Branson, Missouri as his place of business or corporate offices after MWHMC incorporated in May of 2002."

In November of 2005, another interview was conducted with the management of Branson Postal Express at 1316 West Highway 76, Branson, Missouri. This time the interview was conducted with Bobbie, the assistant manager. Same type of operation, these were businesses that were in full operation so we had to speak to the owners and managers whenever and wherever we could. Bobbie was standing behind the counter and stated, "Earlier in the month, Monica Lopez-Rodriguez came into Branson Postal Express with an older white male with white hair, introduced him only as Serguei, she said "Serguei wants his name off of the Application Form for Personal Mail Box 150." Bobbie stated, he said "OKAY," and she completed the new form, and she inserted the name of "Anton Kim." Bobbie stated, "The address provided on the new form was 305 East Walnut, Springfield, Missouri." John and I looked at each other, because we knew that MWHMC has not used that address since August of 2004, over a year ago.

John and I later in the week conducted another interview of Bobbie at Branson Post Express, 1316 West Highway 76, Branson, Missouri. It was the same type of setting, still a business operation and we had to wait for him to get a break from his business to speak to us. When he did, Bobbie reminded us that "Monica had come into the office with Serguei and had filed a new Application Form for the person receiving mail at Personal Mail Box 150." He said, "Monica had failed to provide any identification for Anton Kim and Monica told me that Anton's identification was maintained at the MWHMC office, and she would provide it to me at a later date." Bobbie went on to say, "It was interesting that the person she identified as Serguei did not speak during the entire time that he was there." I then showed Bobbie a picture of Serguei Choukline, and Bobbie identified the photo of Serguei Choukline, saying "That's the person that was introduced to me as Serguei." Bobbie stated that "Serguei has not returned to the Branson Postal Express since taking his name off of the application." John asked Bobbie if they had every conducted any business at the address, like working on computers, on the phone or anything to do with their business. Bobbie responded by saying "At no time have I ever seen Monica Lopez-Rodriguez or Serguei Choukline conducting business, operating computers, or making telephone calls while in the Branson Postal Express store and I have only seen Monica Lopez-Rodriguez picking up mail for MWHMC!" Even though we still have not identified Anton Kim he is still a target for our investigation, but Monica and Serguei have now become the primary targets of this investigation. It is all starting to come together.

Chapter Six

Deep Dive to Arrests

We, John, and I have been travelling back and forth to Springfield, Missouri, staying in a hotel there and doing this sometimes two or three times a month, depending on where the leads take us. It seemed like we should just rent an apartment in the Branson and Springfield, Missouri area as we were traveling there so often. That is the difference in working with the government. That certainly was rough on the family life back in Kansas City as I was gone a lot. We went where the case took us.

Though I transferred to Kansas City in August of 2005, my informants that had been developed in the investigation of Serguei, were transferred as well. Normally, they would be transferred to someone else in the office I left, but since they were important to the investigation of Serguei, they remained under my control. Their control numbers were changed to a Kansas City control number, but they were allowed to continue to reside in the Springfield and Branson area and continued to provide information as it becomes available to them in this case.

We continued to reach out to the hotel and motel owners in Branson, Missouri as that was the focus of attention for Serguei's businesses. Branson is a big tourist attraction especially for the folks that love country music, theme parks, and stage shows. They also had helicopter rides, the duck boats for Lake Taneycomo, and the Show Boat Branson Belle. The Branson Belle has a dinner theater that people buy tickets for, it goes out on the lake, and while they watch the show, eat dinner, or just walked around the deck, the Belle tours around the lake and then returned to the dock to unload. They put on quite a show, the dinner is surprisingly good too!

I digress! I think John and I spoke to every hotel/motel owner in the Branson area. Winter would be coming soon, and the industry would start shutting down for the season, the foreign workers should be returning to their homeland, if Serguei did what he was supposed to.

Though we focused our attention on the Branson, Missouri area, we had a few loose ends to tie up in Springfield, Missouri so let's go there first. In October 2005, we returned to the 305 East Walnut and spoke again to Gina Sharp, Rental Manager for the Vandicort Building. Sharp reiterated the fact that Serguei only rented for a period from November 2002 until April 2004, not quite two years, and that the suite was usually unoccupied except for on occasion with Serguei's wife and an unknown white female. She said that she had never seen any other employees in or visiting the office. Sharp stated that on one occasion she contacted Irina, Serguei's wife who was the only person in the office to remind her that the rent was due. Irina, again the only one in the office, went inside, and returned a few minutes later with the rental check signed by none other than Anton Kim. Sharp then provided us a copy of the check with Anton Kim's signature on a check of MWHMC.

We interviewed the Human Resources Manager for Ozark City Center in Branson, Missouri by the name of Lois Gosh. Gosh was very cooperative, as most of the hotel managers were that we spoke with through this investigation. Why were they so cooperative? Because none of them liked how Serguei treated his employees and how unreliable he was. It was no different with Ozark City Center. They, like most other hotels, employed 10-15 of Serguei's workers and paid Serguei a substantial amount of money, into the tens of thousands of dollars. The checks were either hand delivered to Choukline or sent in the mail.

Gosh told John and I that they stopped using the services of Serguei because of the complaints the management received from the workers. They complained that Serguei wasn't paying them and that they had no money for food and that some of the workers returned to their respective countries without being paid. Gosh said that Serguei had made several promises and just never follow up on them. He was just so unreliable that they terminated his service. Gosh told us she believed one of her employees had been assisting Serguei with his recruitment and was believed to be receiving kickbacks from him as well but was unsure if that was true.

John and I spoke with the Manager of Ozark Mountain Golf Resort, Waterfall Hotel, and the General Manager of the Kings Hotel, which was once called the Goodnight Inn. All of the reports and stories were the same. Terminated services because of the way he [Serguei], treated his employees, paying them less than what was expected, or not paying them at all; mistreatment of the employees, making promises he didn't keep.

All of these employers told us the same, they contacted Monica by way of email or fax, the payroll was faxed to MWHMC and then the checks were sent to MWHMC in the mail for the work completed by the foreign laborers. The manager of Waterfall Hotel said it got so bad, the workers not being paid, and not having shelter, that they provided housing for them at a rate of only $100.00 per month. They all stated that the workers provided a good service and they really felt bad for them. Some of the managers just did not like Serguei. The females that were working for Serguei, were forced to give up their Social Security Cards, and if they refused, they were moved to a different hotel, forced to live in a hotel room with several other girls and were treated very badly.

Serguei would show up periodically with other males and it was implied to the manager of the Waterfall Inn that we were interviewing, that the girls were forced to provide sexual services for these men, or face being sent back to their country. The mal treatment of the workers was not only physical, but mental as well. The workers were forced by Serguei to purchase or buy insurance before being allowed to come to the United States, but they never saw proof of or knowledge of what type of insurance they supposedly purchased. They had to pay Serguei an additional $2,000.00 to come to the United States.

From the information we have received through our investigation, we know that Irina Choukline, Serguei's wife, is involved in the criminal enterprise or scheme as well. The current manager of the Kings Inn said that at one time Irina came to the hotel to surprise Serguei. He became terribly upset with her and sent her home and she was never seen again at the hotel. These managers would tell us stories of Serguei not paying his workers and actually kicking them out on the street with nowhere to go.

Backup a little bit to October 7, 2005, while in Springfield, Missouri, I received a call from the Customs and Border Protection (CBP), out of Minneapolis/St. Paul Airport, Linbergh Terminal, advising that Serguei had just reentered the United States from an overseas business trip. Because of our investigation of Serguei, we had put a lookout in our system, to at least know his foreign travel. The CBP officer stated that he was told by Serguei that he was working as a consultant on International Trade for the last two weeks. The CBP officer provided copies of the documents that were found in his carryon luggage, as his regular luggage had been misrouted and was not available for inspection. One particular document in his luggage was a letter from the International Association of Law Enforcement Intelligence Analyst, providing him access to the organization's website. This bit of information was concerning to us. Here is a person who claims to be Russian Organized Crime, and we know from a previous Source that he was Russian Naval Intelligence. We know he is involved in a current criminal scheme and has been investigated in another criminal scheme; he is not a United States citizen, but a Resident Alien in the United States and is allowed to have been accepted to a class, passed the course, and has been given access to the Law Enforcement Intelligence database. This just seems unbelievable and makes no sense to me at this point. We decided not to contact this intelligence agency for fear of disclosing our own ongoing investigation.

Serguei also had in his possession his Russian Passport, and a Ukrainian Passport in the name of Ruslan Semenchenko, valid from April 2000 until April 2010. He also had a bank card, Social Security Card in the name of Damir Brkanovich. We know who Brkanovich is, he is the purported owner of AAA Hotel Services. But who is Semenchenko? This is a name we haven't heard before. Is this possibly another fictitious name used by Serguei for another phony business?

On October 8, 2005, John, and I, because of the lead from Customs and Border Protection, were able to intercept Serguei when he arrived back in Springfield, Missouri from his business trip abroad. We went to the Springfield, Missouri Airport, badged our way in through security and observed from a distance him being picked up by his wife Irina Choukline. We attempted to follow them from the airport to see where they go. We followed them to their vehicle and began to surveil them. It was late at night and was now raining and I was driving as we, on the spur of the moment, only had us to do the surveillance.

Now I have been doing this for a long time. I am not new at doing surveillance. I have with my years in the gang squad and working drug cases followed some pretty bad individuals and can conduct surveillance I think, pretty well without being detected. This night, I just didn't have my act together. I pulled a real rookie mistake. I forgot to turn on my headlights. I was so concentrated on getting behind them when they pulled out of the parking lot, I didn't turn them on. After a few minutes of making our way through town, John asked "Do you have your headlights on?" I looked down and I did not. I turned them on, and I am sure he [Serguei], saw me as I was only a couple of cars behind him. Hopefully, (I was thinking), he thought it was someone who just forgot to turn their lights on. But again, with his background, his own paranoia, he probably thought the worst. It really did not matter because with the rain and traffic and only having one vehicle, we lost him in traffic.

Since I was now back in Kansas City, I couldn't continue to watch Monica's residence, so I had Michael and Darla, my informants watching and driving by the house periodically and gathering information. On October 9, 2005, for instance, they were able to identify several vehicles found at the residence to include the same minivan registered to MWHMC, and another vehicle, Missouri License 888-WJN, on a 2000 Kia four-dour, registered to Maria Estela Rodriguez, who is known to be Monica Lopez Rodriguez' mother.

On October 18, 2005, I had been advised that the Missouri Department of Labor, Foreign Labor Program, had denied the sixteenth application this time for AAA Hotel Services. There was no approval for MWHMC to change names and keep the same employees. Since the ETA-750 has been denied for visa renewals for AAA Hotel Services Inc. for reasons unknown to me, puts each and every one of MWHMC employees out of status and they must return to their home country, because now they are working for an unapproved employer and without work authorization.

What is an ETA-750? An ETA 750b Form is better known as an Application for Alien Employment Certification. Processed by the US Department of Labor, this form is completed by individuals who live in a foreign country and would like to come to the United States for either temporary or permanent employment. This form requests personal information, job qualifications, and information about the individual's education. The ETA 750b may be used by individual's requesting their first work visa or by individuals already in the US who need to adjust their status.

This investigation has uncovered several email addresses used by MWHMC. These emails, AAAhotelservices@yahoo.com, midwestcorp@yahoo.com and sovteksk@yahoo.com were used by MWHMC, Serguei Choukline, his wife Irina and Monica Lopez-Rodriguez as well as others to conduct business with the employers they supplied workers for. We need to find out what they were saying to each other not only to the employers but to each other. We initially sent yahoo an administrative subpoena from the Department of Homeland Security for the records pertaining to these email addresses. We later followed up with a federal search warrant issued by the United States District Court in Kansas City, Missouri.

Continuing on in October 2005, surveillance was again conducted at the residence of Monica Lopez-Rodriguez several times throughout the month with no change in the vehicles that were observed at her residence. Most of the time, it was her mother's car and the minivan that she drives for MWHMC.

As we continued to interview hotel and motel owners and managers throughout Branson, the story continues to be the same. We were also interviewing citizens of the United States that had supposedly been interviewed and either refused the job offer by MWHMC or were declined to work for the company.

On October 25, 2005, we interview David Harps Jr. who stated that he was hired by an unknown Eastern European and only worked for the company in landscaping, not housekeeping, but only worked for a short time and never met anyone by the name of Monica. He didn't mention the name of Serguei but claimed that he did work for MWHMC.

Another person by the name of Kyle Crowder was interviewed by telephone on October 27, 2005, and said that he lived in Hollister, Missouri. He was out of work for a period of six months and applied for work through the Missouri Unemployment Office and was never interviewed for a job with MWHMC. Crowder stated that he subsequently moved to Las Vegas, NV and is currently employed there. Kyle's name is important because Serguei had to supply names of persons he had interviewed that had not been hired for whatever reason.

We have by this time, identified another email address as mail@mwhmc.com. So now the Department of Homeland Security has sent what is known as a preservation letter to yahoo telling them not to destroy any information associated with these emails in accordance with Title 18, United States Code, Section 2703(f), which states as follows: "…..a provider of wire and electronic communication services or a remote computing service, upon request of a government entity, shall take all necessary steps to preserve records and other evidence in possession pending the issuance of a court order or other process." In other words, they can't destroy any of it!

All through our investigation, we are not only identifying the criminal activity of Serguei Choukline, his wife, and now

Monica Lopez-Rodriguez, we are still trying to identify Anton Kim! We know from our interview of Harps in the past that he did work for MWHMC in landscaping, but this was a new twist for Serguei's operation. So, we pulled the application in which to review it before we talked to Harps again. This time, we met Harps in person, and he told John and I that it was in the middle of 2003 when he applied for a job with MWHMC. He stated that a man by the name of Miguel took him and two others to lunch and discussed employment. Harps said that this person offered him a job in either housekeeping or landscaping. Harps told us that he chose the landscaping job and that he was only there for two or three weeks and was then terminated. Harps was shown a photo lineup that included a photograph of Serguei Choukline. Upon looking at the lineup, Harps identified Serguei Choukline as the person that interviewed him for the job. In the application packet forwarded to the United States Department of Labor in which he stated that he had hired a United States citizen, the packet stated that Anton Kim had interviewed Harps. This application packet for H2B Temporary Workers was one of the visa applications approved in 2003 for eight-nine foreign workers.

On November 15, 2005, John and I traveled to the Ozark Mountain Realty Company and spoke with Daniel Franks, the Property Manager. Franks was given an administrative subpoena to provide rental information as it relates to Monica Lopez-Rodriguez for the period that she resided at 9 Scenic Court, Apartment #9, Branson, Missouri. Franks complied with the subpoena and provided the information. Franks told us that

Monica and Andrew Volkov had abandoned the property in December of 2003.

In following up on information provided in the applications that were submitted to the INS, and other agencies involved for the foreign workers to be supplied by Serguei and MWHMC, we started following up on the supporting documents that was submitted with the applications. Contact was made with Ralph and Jeff Paterson, the previous owners of Goodnight Inn. They were shown photographs that were submitted with the applications that were supposed to be the hotel. Both informed us that they did not have any hotel that looked like the photos submitted. There was also a letter or letters submitted on letterhead from the hotel and they were shown copies of the submitted letters. Both Ralph and Jeff stated they had never submitted or signed any letters for MWHMC, and that the letterhead used was not their letterhead. Both Ralph and Jeff agreed to cooperate in the investigation and provided copies of the contracts completed between them and MWHMC and the signature on the document was that of Anton Kim.

Also in November 2005, Monica Lopez-Rodriguez had come into the Branson Postal Express and wanted to remove the name of Serguei Choukline for the application form of the rental of the P. O. Box 150 and wanted it replaced with the name of Anton Kim. Bobbie Jones, the manager that we had spoken to in the past, provided copies of the latest application form and the name Anton Kim was listed, and his address was identified as 305 East Walnut Street, Springfield, Missouri which had not been used for over a year.

Later in November of 2005, contact was again made with Gina Sharp as it relates to the address of 305 East Walnut, Suite 305, Springfield, Missouri. John and I needed to speak to Sharp in relation to a letter that was supposedly completed by her to be submitted with the applications for more H2B workers for MWHMC. Sharp, in this instance, stated that she did complete and provide the letter. She said that she had a practice of doing this if the tenant was a good tenant and paid on time.

In December 2005, I was informed by the Kansas City office that a citizen and national of Bulgaria was in custody and based on information in his file, he had resided in Branson, Missouri and possibly worked for Serguei Choukline and MWHMC. John and I made arrangements to have him brought into the Detention Unit to be interviewed.

Mihail Stoyanov Mihaylov was then taken to my office where he was interviewed. The story is much like the same as all of the other workers that Serguei misused and abused. He said that he entered the United States on June 6, 2003, as a J-1 Exchange Visitor who was authorized to remain in the United States until August 17, 2003. He said that he overstayed his visa and was now in deportation proceedings.

Mihaylov told us that when he first entered the United States, he was employed at the Hillside Christian Camp as a fencing instructor, He stated that he left their employment after the date that he was supposed to return to his country. He stated that he then, with his girlfriend at the time, Borgania Afar, came to Branson, Missouri. Afar had a friend that told her about a guy in Branson by the name of Serguei who could help him find a job. He said he gave his girlfriend copies of his passport and travel documents, and she gave them to Serguei. He told us that he arrived in Branson in the first part of September of 2003 and soon after meeting Serguei, began employment at the Motel 9 in Branson, Missouri. Mihaylov said that he left after working there for a year and went to Chicago and then returned to Branson in April of 2005.

Mihaylov stated that he never met Serguei. He told us the same as everyone else if he had payroll issues or problems contact Monica. Like all of the others, Mihaylov stated that his biggest complaint with Serguei's company was that sometimes he didn't get his paycheck for two or three weeks. He would call Monica, who as before, said she would check on it and a couple of days later, he would get paid. He then said that when he did get paid, he would find that his check had been shorted twenty to thirty dollars. He said he was told by other workers that he had to pay this to work for Serguei.

Mihaylov said that he believed that Monica was signing the paychecks, but he wasn't sure. He told us however, he could have been paid by money order, but no matter what the case, he didn't deal with anyone but Monica.

In the first part of December 2005, John and I made contact with Nina Lancer, the owner of the We Box It, 3000 Green Mountain Drive, Branson, Missouri. Lancer told us that she has owned the We Box It since about August of 2004, so by this time, just over a year. Lancer told us that Personal Mail Box #124 was registered to several individuals and companies. The application listed Evgenia Urazova, Alexander Urazov and

J and J Group International. She stated that another person listed as receiving mail in box 124 was Monica Lopez and AAA Hotel Services Inc. Lancer added that the mail box was rented in January of 2004. We wondered if J and J Group International was the next phony business associated with Serguei.

Lancer informed us that the person she dealt with was Monica Lopez, and she is the one who picks up the mail. Lancer said she has seen mail come from Flowers Inn, and The Hacienda. Lancer stated that the checks that she has seen made out by Monica were on AAA Hotel Services checks. Lancer said she asked Monica one time where she worked or what kind of work she did, and Monica told her she brings in kids from overseas to the United States and places them in jobs. Lancer said she did know that Monica recently purchased a new vehicle and believed it to be a small brown Ford Focus.

On December 19, 2005, I submitted an affidavit to the United States District Court for the Western District of Missouri in Kansas City, Missouri for a search warrant for the yahoo email accounts that we have identified as associated with this investigation. Those emails are as previously identified AAAhotelservices@yahoo.com, midwestcorp@yahoo.com, sovtek@yahoo.com and mail@mwhmc.com and any other emails associated with Serguei Choukline's home address in conjunction with violations of law associated with visa fraud, money laundering, false statements, and mail fraud.

Information recovered from the yahoo search warrant revealed several things. We were able to determine that there were other businesses besides MWHMC and AAA Hotel Services like

J and J, that Serguei was trying to use to supply foreign workers to businesses in and around Branson and Springfield, Missouri. We were able to find that Serguei Choukline was attempting to obtain status in the Slovakian Republic and may be married to a citizen of Slovakia, as well as his wife Irina in the United States. Further information obtained were in emails received from Irina Choukline reminding Monica Lopez who Anton Kim is and that she is not to use names in conversations and if people want to reach Anton Kim, they are to contact him at the email address of mail@mwhmc.com. There was another email from Serguei Choukline to his wife Irina telling her to write checks under the name of Anton Kim, and how to move it through the different bank accounts relating to Sovtek Corporation and AAA Hotel Services. There were many other emails recovered dealing with the payroll of his employees as well as other business operations associated with Serguei and MWHMC.

Based on the information that we obtained from the yahoo search warrant, along with all of the interviews that have been conducted, surveillances of both Serguei and Monica, it was time to take this investigation from the somewhat covert phase to the search and arrest phase.

On January 10, 2006, a Grand Jury was held in the United States District Court for the Western District of Missouri at Kansas City for charges against, to start with, Monica Lopez-Rodriguez. Upon completion of my testimony before the Grand Jury, where our case is laid out before them, Monica Lopez-Rodriguez was indicted (charged), with two counts of False Statements in violation of 18, USC, 1001: two counts of mail fraud in violation of 18 USC 1341, and two counts of Visa Fraud in violation of 18, USC 1546. Upon completion of the Grand Jury testimony, I filed an affidavit for a search warrant to search Monica's home address of 111 Crosby Street, Branson, Missouri as well as search any computers and components she may have in the residence. The warrant was subsequently approved by the judge. Now it is time to put in the agency request for the operation and the manpower needed.

I immediately completed the operations plan, requesting manpower to travel to Springfield, get motel rooms for all attending, equipment needed: radios, firearm, vests, search equipment like bags, evidence tape, all of the essentials. Should we contact the Branson, Missouri Police Department for assistance, as it was told that Serguei may have friends at the Police Department. It was decided to wait until just before we executed to tell them we were going in. Nothing against the Police Department or it's fine officers that put their lives on the line each and every day, but we needed to make sure nothing went wrong, this case has taken too long. The operations plan was approved, the agents that would be assisting would be briefed the day before, photographs of the address and Monica had already been taken from our previous surveillances. We were ready to go!

On January 18, 2006, all of the HSI agents that were participating as well as the agents from the United States Department of Labor that were assisting in the search and arrest traveled to Springfield, Missouri. We all got checked into our hotels and then traveled to my old Springfield, Missouri Office and met the agents there that would be participating in the execution of the search and arrest warrants. There were probably about ten of us total that were going to execute the warrant. You hear a lot about the number of agents and officers executing a particular search warrant as being over bearing or to many, but to be honest, the more that are there, depending on the size of the residence the safer it is, the quicker the search is completed, and we can get in and out as quick as possible.

We went to the HSI Office in Springfield and held a second briefing and agreed that the best time to execute the warrant was about 7:00 AM. This is a time that we knew that Monica would be home. It was decided to meet again at the HSI Office at 5:00 AM on January 19, 2006. We would depart from there and drive the 45 minutes to Branson, Missouri (with everybody's driving habits being different and not knowing the traffic going south out of Springfield at that time of the morning), we wanted to allow everyone ample time to get to the staging site. After everyone was ready to go, we would leave at about 5:45 AM and would meet in the parking lot of a grocery store near the address.

The day is here! We met at the HSI Office as planned, opened the office, had some coffee, I think I even picked up donuts, double checked our equipment, made sure everything was operational, went over the op again and departed on time. We, especially John and I are hyped up, ready to go. We have been at this a long time and were now nearing the end of the investigation. I can't imagine a longer investigation and how those agents must have felt and the anticipation they would have had. We knew Monica was not a high threat target, we did not expect her to start shooting when we entered the door, we knew that we didn't have to make a dynamic entry, that means, knock, and announce and if there is no answer in a short time that we kick the door in or break it down with a ram. We do still have to protect ourselves and she could still surprise us, we don't know who would be in the house when we arrive. We arrived at the secondary stop before moving to the residence to execute the search warrant. David Barnes, the United States Attorney, went to Springfield with us, but would be stationed at the United States Attorney's Office in Springfield to assist as needed as we did not know where this would lead.

At about 6:50 AM we called the Branson Missouri Police Department and informed them what we were doing and then departed in tandem headed for the address of 111 Crosby Street Branson, Missouri. We arrived at the residence on time and surrounded the residence as a necessary precaution, for our safety John and I went to the front door of the residence of Monica Lopez-Rodriguez, knocked on the door and yelled "Police Search Warrant!" Monica came to the door. She was a small Hispanic female, with long dark hair, and was holding her three-year-old child on her hip, her mother, probably in her fifties was on the couch and her brother was in the bedroom in bed. I informed Monica who we were and why we were there as other agents continued to enter the house and conduct a protective sweep of the residence. Make sure everyone is out of their respective room and brought into the living room. For our safety, everyone is patted down to make sure there are no weapons that can be turned on us. Since we knew there were females in the residence, we made sure there was a female agent along as we did not want any accusations of any inappropriate activity. A guard if you will, would be posted in the living room with them for our safety and the other agents began to search.

Monica was in tears, her mother and brother were upset and crying, wondering what was going on. Everyone in the residence was first interviewed as to their immigration status in the United States. It was determined that Monica's mother, Maria Elena Rodriguez and brother, Luis Lopez-Rodriguez were in violation of their immigration status because they were in the United States on B-2, visitor for pleasure visas and failed to return to Mexico when required.

As the other agents conducted the search of the residence, John and I sat down with Monica and explained that we also had a warrant for her arrest for false statements, visa fraud and mail fraud. We advised her of her appropriate Miranda Rights and told her that we would like to speak to her, but she did not have to without an attorney present as identified in the rights that we had read to her. Monica stated that she wanted to speak to us and provided the following information:

Monica said she was a citizen and national of Mexico and a Resident Alien in the United States. (The actual application for Resident Alien Status had not yet been approved). Monica and her husband Andrea Volkov were married in 2000 in Harrison, Arkansas. She went with him to Russia in 2002 and was only there for a short period of time, probably for a total of about six months. Her whole purpose for being there was to learn the Russian language. She lived in several different places while she was there but could not find work.

Monica continued on to say she never attended any kind of school in Russia, nor did she ever obtain a bachelor's degree from a college in Russia. She never worked for Sovtek Corporations or any other parent company of MWHMC at any time in Russia as had been said in her own visa application filed by MWHMC and Serguei. She returned to the United States because she did not like Russia and could not find work.

Monica said she returned to the United States and Serguei hired her to work for him knowing that she was in the United States on a B-2, Nonimmigrant Visitor for Pleasure visa, and did not have work authorization. Lopez said that she was hired because of her language skills in Spanish and Russian. Serguei had her sign all of the paperwork for AAA Hotel Services Inc as the registered agent telling her it was because she was the agent in the area. He [Serguei] gave her a company credit card and told her what she could and couldn't use it for.

Serguei kept telling her that he was no longer an employee of MWHMC, and his name needed to come off of the records at the Branson Postal Express in Branson, so he went with her to the office to remove his name, but the person at the office, wanted an identification from Anton Kim whose name she was trying to list for the box. She said that she as others believe that Serguei is Anton Kim, but she did not question it because she wanted to keep her job.

Serguei, even though he supposedly was no longer employed by MWHMC, still continued to give her advice on how to handle employee issues and tells her everything that she has to do. Serguei continued to tell her that she is on the paperwork for AAA Hotel Services Inc, that she is in control. Monica still handles all of the payroll and would then take the paperwork to Irina Choukline, Serguei's wife for her to complete the payroll. She would take them to her house on West Suzanne Place, in Springfield, Missouri but if she sees Serguei, she will give them to him. The last time she was at Serguei's residence was about two weeks prior to drop off mail and reports for the businesses.

When she first started working for Serguei, there was another Russian female there by the name of Anya Bauer who did the same work she did. Anya had more responsibility such as signing different documents, picking up rent and attending meetings with Serguei. When Anya worked for the company, she did all of the interviews of the United States applicants and did the payroll before Irina Choukline started doing it. Anya worked out of the office on Walnut Street in Springfield, Missouri. We have now possibly identified the other white female that was seen in the office with Serguei's wife Irina.

Monica said she does not know who Damir Brkanovich is and has never met him. Even when the paperwork for AAA Hotel Services Inc was signed, he was not there, it was only Serguei, and he is the one that told her to sign the paperwork. As far as Monica knows, Serguei Choukline is the boss. Monica said that Serguei has his business at his residence and keeps his records on computers to include a laptop and several filing cabinets. She said one time she was given a stack of papers to sign by Serguei as it related to her visa application and was told to provide copies of her passport, visa, and other paperwork to submit with the application for her status in the United

States. She said she knew that there were false statements in the application that related to her education, employment, and residences during the last several years, but she was told by Serguei to sign it and the company would file the application on her behalf.

Serguei was out of the country a lot and she dealt with the employees. She knew that Serguei had another wife in Slovakia by the name of Martina Pirohova. She [Pirohova] had come to the United States on a J-1 Exchange Visitor visa and Serguei had an affair with her during that time. To the best of her knowledge, they are still married, and she lives in Slovakia and Serguei lives in the United States with his wife here, Irina.

This completed our interview with Monica, and it certainly cleared up a lot of questions that we have about the operation of the business, where it is located and who Anton Kim is. It appears that we were all correct in our assumptions that Serguei Choukline and Anton Kim and Damir Brkanovich are all one in the same. Also, to understand how she came to speak Russian, and that she had indeed traveled to and lived in Russia which was truly a surprise to us.

By this time, the execution of the search warrant of Monica's residence was complete. Monica's mother and brother were transported to the HSI Office in Springfield, Missouri for processing. Both were placed in removal proceedings for overstaying their visitor visas, but instead of being held on bond, they were released on their own recognizance to take care of Monica's three-year-old son. Monica was taken into custody on the arrest warrant and was transported by John and me to the United States Court House in Springfield, Missouri and was turned over to the United States Marshal Service to be processed for the arrest and to appear for her first appearance before the judge later in the afternoon.

  This has been a busy day already. I don't remember what time it was when we finished, but I think by the time we executed the arrest and search warrant on Monica's home, the interview, transfer of evidence, which included three computers to the office in Springfield to be placed in the evidence room, and transport of everyone it was probably about noon. We went to lunch with the AUSA Barnes and discussed our next step. We had to be back by early afternoon because Monica Lopez-Rodriguez had her first appearance soon. She, [Monica] was held in custody, because due to her immigration status being obtained by fraud, I placed a detainer with the United States Marshal Service, stating that if she was to be released, we wanted to take custody of her to be placed in removal proceeding for visa fraud.

  After the initial appearance of Monica, we sat down with AUSA Barnes and began to work on an affidavit for a complaint in the Western District of Missouri in the Southern Division at Springfield, Missouri to charge Serguei with one count of a violation of Title 18, USC 371, Conspiracy to commit Visa Fraud in violation of 18, USC 1546. This would cause the issuance of an arrest warrant for him, and then a second affidavit was completed for a search warrant to search his residence on West Suzanne Place in Springfield, Missouri. The information that Monica provided in her interview along with the evidence and statements we had collected throughout this investigation, we believed that we had ample evidence to get the charges and the warrant for Serguei. We did! Later that afternoon, probably about four O'clock, an arrest warrant was issued for Serguei D. Choukline for a violation of 18, USC 371 Conspiracy, along with the issuance of a search warrant for his residence.

The only problem is, we can't wait until tomorrow. Serguei probably already knows that Monica has been arrested and her house has been searched. We are sure that he knows he is next, and how much evidence has he already destroyed, has he absconded or left town were our questions. No, we can't wait, we need to go tonight! Here we go again. This is going to be an awfully long day.

We had warrants in hand, we still had agents there from Kansas City HSI, United States Department of Labor and agents from the Springfield HSI Office available to assist. Our local agency that we would be dealing with was the Greene County Missouri Sheriff's Office located there in Springfield, Missouri, due to the fact that though Serguei's residence has a Springfield, Missouri address, it is actually located out in the county. We went back to the Springfield HSI Office and typed out the Operation Plan to search Serguei's residence and execute the arrest and search warrants at the late hour of 7:00 PM. You remember we executed Monica's warrants at 7:00 AM so it has already been a long day. We submitted the request for the operation to Kansas City and were waiting for the approval. In the meantime, we contacted all of the agents that were to assist and the Greene County Sheriff's Office for assistance and asked for a couple of deputies to help us execute a search and arrest warrant. We all met at the Springfield HSI Office for a briefing on the operation at 6:00 PM. We thought we would surely have the approval from Kansas City back by then.

It was now 6:00 PM and everyone is present for the briefing. The only thing we don't have is the approval from Kansas City yet. You remember earlier in the first investigation where I identified the retired Army Intelligence Officer who had been in Serguei's residence and provided me a map of the interior of his house. Well, I still had the map from the other case file, and I had it with me. I was able to describe to everyone assisting exactly what they would be going into. We knew where the living room was with the fireplace with the Russian Crest hanging on it, the storm room with all of the file cabinets and where Irina's work space was downstairs in the family room in a cutout area under the steps. We also knew where Serguei's office was and where he would most likely be. We, with the assistance of the Greene County Sheriff's deputies identified a staging location only a few blocks from Serguei's residence where we would all meet and go in together. Remember the description of where Serguei's home is, at the end of a Cul-de-Sac, with only one way in and one way out, with this parade of all of our vehicles, we are going to cause quite a commotion.

Just as it was described by the Russian arrest team that arrested Serguei in Russia, we too had heard of his military experience, we knew or suspected that he had been training with John Irish from the first investigation in martial arts or in boxing. By information we had received from our previous informant, he was Russian Naval Intelligence, and by his own claims, he was involved in Russian Organized Crime. Is this all narcissism on Serguei's part, or was he really involved in these activities? Was he always armed as we had heard during our investigation of Serguei or is it just claims he made to make himself look important. We don't know and we can't take any chances. How does the story go? "Hope for the best, but plan for the worst," and that is what we had to do in this situation.

We were all ready to go, but the final approval had not yet arrived. We were getting close to our go time, so John and I sent everyone to the staging point to include AUSA Barnes. Yes, this time AUSA Barnes was with us and was actually going to the operation location. He stated that he could not go inside the residence, but he could go and standby on the outside of the residence. John and I waited at the office for the faxed approval of the operation. It was about 6:40 PM when the approval finally came in, we jumped in my vehicle and headed toward the staging location. We had already radioed everyone and let them know that we had the approval and were on our way. As we were headed south on Missouri State Highway 65, south of Interstate 44, we hit traffic that was at a standstill. Are you kidding me, this could not have come at a worse time. We looked at each other and turned on the emergency lights and siren and took to the shoulder of the highway to get past the slowed traffic.

We met everyone at the staging location which was a church parking lot just a few blocks away from Serguei's neighborhood, rechecked all of our gear, radios, vests, entry tool should it be necessary, and we departed. I think we had about six or eight vehicles including the sheriff patrol vehicles, we all stacked up or lined up if you will, with John and I at the front of the line. We also had a couple of our agents with long-guns and at least one of the four sheriff deputies had a long-gun as we lined up at the front door. We paused for a second, looked at each other and said, "here we go!"

Knocking on the door yelling "Police, Search Warrant, Open the Door!" We said this a couple of times as we were getting ready to breach the door with a ram and all of a sudden, the door slowly opened! There was an older woman, probably in her late 70's or early 80's that opened the door, turned, and walked away. As we all quickly piled into the residence, not knowing what we are going to encounter, she just walked back to her seat on the couch and sat down. I instructed one of the agents to watch her and watch the door as the rest of us proceeded through the house conducting a sweep of the residence yelling "Police Search Warrant; Police Search Warrant," but there were no answers. Was there no one else at home? Was everyone gone? Everyone went in the direction they were instructed to go at the briefing, and John and I headed downstairs to where we knew Serguei's office to be. We got to the bottom of the steps and saw the open storm room with file cabinets, we rounded the corner and saw a seating area and Irina's work space under the steps. There was no one else downstairs that we could see.

As we approached Serguei's office, we could hear what sounded like him typing on his computer and some sort of explosion. As we got closer to the door, we could see Serguei sitting at his desk, with his back toward the door, frantically typing on his computer with noises of some sort from the computer that I could not make out. I yelled "Serguei, stop" "Stop typing" "Stop what you're doing, get away from the computer." but he continued, without stopping. I was remembering my fears of him destroying evidence as Monica had told us that a lot of his business files are located on his computer and laptop. It almost seemed like he was ignoring me, refusing to obey a command to stop. Serguei had on a shirt and a blue jean jacket as I could see the shirt collar up over the back of the jean jacket. John was behind me, standing at the office door providing security as I stepped closer into the room and closer to Serguei. I ran up to the back of Serguei and grabbed him by the back of the collar of his shirt and blue jean jacket and pulled him, with a substantial amount of force, out of his chair and away from the computer just as a loud noise came from the computer that sounded like an explosion. Serguei yelled in Russian something I am sure was not very nice and since I don't speak Russian, I can only imagine what he said. Serguei was thrown to the ground face first onto the floor and my gun was put at the back of his neck, just as John, my co-case agent and partner in this investigation and I got on top of Serguei. He [Serguei] was continuing to struggle until I yelled "Serguei, stop! It's Stoker with Immigration, stop fighting!" He then stopped fighting, turned, and looked at me and relaxed as John and I handcuffed him. We picked him up and were preparing to take him upstairs to the dining room table to interview him. I looked around to see what he was doing at his computer. Was he destroying evidence or what. It turned out he had a set of earbuds in his ears and was playing a video war game on the computer and didn't hear a word I said! As the explosion on the game came, in his eyes, it probably appeared that he was being blown out of the chair. I am sure that was an experience that he wasn't expecting in his game! Serguei was taken upstairs, and John and I sat him down at the dining room table. We sat across from him and began our interview.

We first explained to Serguei that we had a warrant for his arrest for the offense of conspiracy to commit visa fraud and also had a search warrant to search his home for evidence of that crime. We also told him that we had already arrested Monica Lopez and searched her residence as well. We informed him that we had enough to charge him and his wife Irina with these offenses, but, if he is willing to tell us about these charges, we would like to hear what he had to say. Before we went any further, we needed to read him his appropriate Miranda Warning, which we did. We asked him again if he wanted to talk to us about all MWHMC, the applications for the H2B workers and Anton Kim. He commences to say that he knew that we had been watching him and that we had been following him all over the city. I told him, that we had not followed him and if he had someone following him there was another problem because it was not us. I reiterated the fact that we knew that Irina was involved in the crimes as well and that as of this moment, he and Monica were the only people that were charged with anything. He looked at me and John and said, "I don't want to say anything, I want an attorney!" That was my queue that I had to stop. John and I ceased our questioning and left him sitting at the dining room table with an agent watching him and we began to assist the others in the execution of the search warrant.

As we were in the middle of conducting our search or Serguei's residence, I was called to the down stair's family room where laying on top of the pool table and spread out from one side to the other were a large number of long rifles. I was asked what we should do with them. They were not named in the items to be searched for and Serguei was a Lawful Permanent Resident in the United States and could therefore own the weapons. I had to tell the other agents searching to leave them there. I was also directed to the storm room at the bottom of the steps going into the basement. Inside the storm room were several four drawer file cabinets full of documentation associated with MWHMC, AAA Hotel Services Inc and all of the applications that had been filed by Serguei and his businesses for H2B foreign laborers. We emptied the drawers of all relevant paperwork and boxed it up as evidence.

As we continued the search, I was called to the work area under the steps in the family room used by Irina Choukline to do payroll for MWHMC, SOVTEK Corporation and AAA Hotel Services Inc. Items found in, on and around the desk were payroll records associated with current employees of these companies. Upon completion of the search warrant, several boxes of documents associated with the businesses were seized as well as travel documents, payroll documents, several computers, and a closed and locked brief case. One of the applications recovered was the visa application for Monica Lopez-Rodriguez.

Serguei was arrested and transported to the Greene County Jail where he was housed until he could be picked up the following day and transported to the United States Marshal Service to be processed by them and attend his first appearance before the United States Magistrate Judge. The evidence was transported to the HSI Office, Springfield, Missouri where it would be housed until it could be transported to the HSI Office, Kansas City, Missouri.

Serguei was transported on January 20, 2006, to the United States Marshal Service, Springfield, Missouri for processing and booked as a United States Marshal prisoner. On January 23, 2006, he appeared before United States Magistrate Judge, James England. The initial appearance is basically for the judge to assure that Serguei has a copy of the complaint filed against him and that he understands his rights under the law. Serguei stated that he understood everything that was explained to him. A detention hearing was scheduled for January 31, 2006, at 11:30 AM. Serguei was remanded to United State Marshal's custody.

I had to be present at the hearing as I was told by AUSA Barnes to be prepared to testify because based on the information we had received, he [Barnes] was going to the request for detention without bond for Serguei due to his contacts outside of the United States and being a potential flight risk. I testified to the weapons, gas mask and knives found at his residence, his extensive travel abroad over the last couple of years, as well as passports from Poland and Slovakia. Based on what Monica Lopez-Rodriguez had told us about a potential wife in Slovakia, this information was disclosed as well.

After my testimony, Judge England stated he would take the information under advisement and rule on a later date. As he said he would do, Judge England ruled on February 2, 2006, that Serguei would be released on a $50,000.00 Bond and as a part of that release, he had to report to pre-trial services three days per week. Serguei posted the bond and was released pending further court appearances.

Chapter Seven

Evidence and Charges

We've done search warrants on Monica's residence and Serguei's residence, our two main targets of this investigation have been identified. As we developed these two individuals, we've identified a few others in the process. We've identified Serguei's wife, Irina Choukline, she is purported to be the bookkeeper and based on the information that was provided to us by Monica and what was found during the search warrant of her work area in the Choukline residence, she was indeed involved. We have identified Anya Bauer, a person who was hired by Serguei in the beginning of the fraud scheme, and per Monica, traveled with Serguei to meetings and was doing her job with hiring the foreign labor force before she arrived. Then there is Agnieska Koblenc, another person who had been applied for by Serguei in 2004 not only once, but twice to enter the United States as an L1A Intracompany Transferee. Lastly, the last person that seems to be a part of this criminal scheme is Irina Lemetyuynen who was applied for in 2003, also as an L1A Intracompany Transferee for MWHMC.

You think that after the search and arrest warrants are executed, the case is over and we move into the court phase of the investigation, well that is not the case. You have to gather the evidence recovered during the search warrants; it has to be reviewed. Monica gave us a statement and provided some pretty damaging information and that had to be deciphered and the truthfulness of the statement has to be verified. As we conducted the search warrants and recovered the evidence at Serguei's residence we recovered a lot of information relating to other businesses and companies that he had done business with. All of this has to be gone through and verified.

As we reviewed the evidence recovered during the two search warrants, we found a lot of additional information. In Serguei's house, we also recovered a locked brief case, that a separate search warrant will be applied for at a later time to open it. We did find a receipt for the amount of money spent by Serguei for a marriage license in Eureka Springs, Arkansas. I am guessing that was for him and Martina Pirohova to get married in Eureka Springs, Arkansas, not Harrison, Arkansas as we had initially been told, as well as a copy of an identification card from the Slovakian Republic in the name of Sergey Shuklin, the Slovakia spelling of his name.

We recovered several computers that will be sent off for forensics review, but also recovered were letters from the Nebraska Service Center in Lincoln, NE, which were actually determined to be fraudulent. There was an email from Serguei Choukline to Martina Pirohova telling her to write a letter to the Slovakian government telling them that her husband, Sergey Shuklin will not be a burden on the Slovakian Social System when he moves to Slovakia to reside with her at her address and that she will be able to provide substantial support for him. He told her the letter needed to be notarized. What is interesting, is that the letter and the notary stamps, were both found in Serguei's possession. There was a list of items found in his possession of the main things to be moved to Slovakia from the United States. There was also a copy of the official seal of the Department of Homeland Security.

After seeing the receipt for the marriage license, I contacted the Circuit Clerk from Carroll County Arkansas and verified that Serguei Choukline and Martina Pirohova were married in Carroll County Arkansas on August 5, 2003. Further records checks revealed that Serguei is also identified as the President/CEO of the Russian Chamber of Commerce in the European Union, located at his address of Stefanikova 42, 040 01 Kosice, Slovakia. If you remember during our interview of Monica, she advised that while she was in Russia, she had visited the home that he shared with Martina Pirohova and her parents. This information certainly leads us to believe that Serguei Choukline is attempting to get his affairs in order to leave the United States and travel to Slovakia to reside with his wife Martina Pirohova.

We identified another company that had done business with Serguei as Jupiter Properties in Branson, Missouri. The General Manager of the company, Javier Simions was interviewed as to his working relationship with Serguei Choukline and MWHMC. Simions stated that he had done business with MWHMC and that he had signed a contract with Serguei, and Serguei signed the contract in his presence, but when he got the contract, it had the name of Anton Kim. Simions said that he had never met Anton Kim. He said that the checks for the rooms rented for the employees of MWHMC always came quickly.

Simions said that Serguei introduced him to Betty Hunter. He said he had only met her once, but she was the person that directed him to mail the checks to the address in Springfield, Missouri. Simions said that he really did not know if MWHMC provided H2B workers to both of his hotels, but he did get a lot of complaints from the employees that he did have from MWHMC. One complaint was, that they were charged too much to stay at the hotel and they weren't making enough to eat, and the Red Cross had to help them get food.

Simions said that at first, it was either Monica Lopez or Anya Bauer who drove the van that transported the workers to work. MWHMC kept a white van at the hotel. After Monica Lopez and Anya Bauer stopped, Pete and Bonnie Johnson drove the van and were paid so much per person to transport them to work. Monica then began to pick up the paychecks, or he mailed them to Springfield.

On February 6, 2006, I filed and affidavit for a search warrant to open the black corolla brief case that was found during the search warrant executed at Serguei's residence. The briefcase had been found in the downstairs office where Serguei was found at the time of his arrest. Because the briefcase was secured, and there was no authorization to enter locked items in our search warrant, so we had to file an affidavit for an additional search warrant to open it. The warrant was granted on the same date and the briefcase was opened. Found inside was the following.

We found copies of a Slovakian Republic driver license in the name of Sergey Shuklin, divorce papers relating to Mark and Christine Bauer, a copy of the criminal history of Serguei Choukline, and copies of letters to be sent to the Slovakian Republic. There were paychecks and documents relating to the tax and income of Martina Pirohova and records identifying Sovtek SK as doing business in the Slovak Republic. Further information to lead us to believe that Serguei may be a flight risk and will attempt to leave the United States.

On February 15, 2006, through the evidence we recovered during our search warrants, we were able to identify the Hinton Inn, in Bentonville, Arkansas as another place the Serguei Choukline through MWHMC was supplying H2B workers to. We now know that he was not limiting his activity to Missouri but had expanded into Arkansas. The owner of the Hotel, Tom Thomas (Tom), stated that he had only used MWHMC for one season at four different properties and that was in 2003. Tom said that he dealt with Serguei and a blond, white female who he believed had a Russian accent, and an unknown Hispanic female. Tom said that he had South Koreans working at his properties but did not know whether they entered the United States as H2B Temporary Workers or J-1 Exchange Visitors. Tom said the workers had told him that they had to return to their country in three or four months.

Tom said that the workers were paid $3.50 to $4.00 per hour, and he provided rooms to them. He went on to say that one of them who he believed his name to be "Kim," had a driver license and transported the workers to and from work. Tom stated that Kim was involved in a traffic accident either in Bentonville or Rogers, Arkansas. Tom, as all of the other owners and managers of hotels and businesses stated that he never gave

Serguei Choukline permission to use any of the addresses of his hotels as a corporate office address. The General Manager, Ms. Downs, stated that she did not like dealing with Serguei, because he was very rude, and always in her face.

On February 16, 2006, John and I traveled to the Arkansas Department of Revenue and spoke with the Assistant Manager, Robbie Moss as it relates to the 1993 Ford Aerostar minivan registered to MWHMC. Moss provided a copy of the Bill of Sale which was signed on the front and on the back by Serguei Choukline, the name of Anton Kim appeared on the vehicle Registration which was completed a week later in the State of Arkansas. We contacted corporal Cayley Cranson of the Rogers, Arkansas Police Department who provided a copy of the Police Report relating to the traffic accident which occurred on April 23, 2003, involving the minivan belonging to MWHMC. The driver of the vehicle was identified as Hong Seok and listed Serguei Choukline as a witness to the accident.

Is this Anton Kim? Is Kim just a name that Serguei called Hong Seok because he could not pronounce his name properly? Kim is the name that was used by Tom because that is what he was told his name was by Serguei, but it does not appear that was his real name. Did Serguei give Hong Seok the name of Anton Kim, and then use it himself in his businesses? These are all questions that we hope we will get to ask Serguei at some point in time.

Later on, the same day, John and I interviewed Linda Cook, General Manager and Joanie Edelweiss, Assistant Manager of The Columns, Branson, Missouri. Both admitted that they used the services of MWHMC in August of 2004 and paid them approximately $2,940.25 for the services provided. They both stated that they did not use the services of MWHMC after that because there were problems with how MWHMC cared for their employees. They said they believed that MWHMC changed their name to AAA Hotel Service in about July 2004.

As we reviewed information that we had received and our reports, we recovered a report of an interview of Richard Kline, Investigator for the Department of Employment Security for the State of Missouri from December 29, 2005, in which Kline provided information relating to wages reported by Irina Lemetyuynen.

Kline said MWHMC filed a petition for nonimmigrant worker on behalf of Lemetyuynen as the Vice President of Technical Support for MWHMC, and that petition was approved and valid from November 2002 until November 4, 2005. In July of 2005 MWHMC filed an Immigrant Petition for Alien worker again for Irina Lemetyuynen claiming that she was still employed by MWHMC as the Vice President of Technical Services. In Support of the application, Anton Kim, Vice President of MWHMC sent a letter dated July 6, 2005, claiming that Irina Lemetyuynen was still employed by MWHMC as the Vice President of Technical Support. That petition was also approved on August 31, 2005, and she was granted Resident Alien status in the United States based on her employment with MWHMC. Kline stated based on a nationwide records search, there has been no earnings reported from Irina Lemetyuynen from the second quarter of 2004 through the third quarter of 2005.

All through the follow up investigation after the arrests of Monica Lopez and Serguei Choukline, the office of the United States Attorney, AUSA David Barnes has been in contact with the attorney of Monica Lopez-Rodriguez to offer her a plea deal to a lesser charge, but in order to do that she had to provide us an additional interview, usually conducted by the investigating agents. On May 12, 2006, that interview with Monica Lopez-Rodriguez took place at the office of the United States Marshal Service, Kansas City, Missouri. Those that were present during the interview of course was Monica, her attorney, John Cress with the United States Department of Labor, and me from the Department of Homeland Security. During the interview, Monica Lopez-Rodriguez provided the following information as it relates to Serguei Choukline and his business operations and her part in the different companies.

Monica reiterated much of what she had already told us during her first interview after being read her Miranda Rights at the time of her arrest. She wanted to add a few things during this interview that she had not previously told us of. We told her to go ahead and tell us her story. She informed us that after she started working for MWHMC she did indeed make deposits in the banking account for the company, and her husband did the driving. Anya Bauer was taking care of most of the payroll. Monica stated that she was the signor on the bank account for AAA Hotel Services Inc, but she did not know the supposed owner, Damir Brkanovich. She went on to say that she never worked with him, nor did she ever meet him.

Monica told us that Serguei took her to downtown Springfield, Missouri and told her that they were opening a company. She said a lady brought them the paperwork and she signed it, and Serguei told her she would be the Secretary of the company. Serguei then told her that he would take the paperwork to the bosses or the attorney to complete the paperwork. Monica said that she and Serguei then went to the bank and opened a bank account. She said that she signed the paperwork at the bank and believed that Serguei signed it also. She said the account was opened in the name of Damir Brkanovich. Monica said the purpose of her signing was so that she could withdraw funds from the account.

Monica was asked why MWHMC changed the name to AAA Hotel Services Inc., and she stated that "Serguei liked playing James Bond." "He likes to make everything look suspicious." "He likes playing spy or something."

Monica said that as far as Anton Kim, she never met him, nor does she know who he is other than the description she was given by Serguei Choukline as an Asian male about fifty years old. She said that when she would get calls from the businesses that she dealt with asking for Anton Kim, Serguei told her to say, "Anton Kim isn't here, he was in New York or Florida." Monica said that she was told to use the name of Anton Kim a lot. She said, she was told to lie a lot.

Monica told us that when she returned to the United States from Russia, is when she began to believe that Serguei Choukline and Anton Kim were one in the same. Serguei is her boss, the one who told her what to do, and Irina Choukline, Serguei's wife is the one who did the payroll.

She went on to say, that Anya Bauer was more involved in dealing with a girl named "Elena." Anya Bauer used to be the person to handle all of the payroll issues, but after she left, Irina Choukline now handles all of the payroll issues. If there is a problem with payroll, she contacts Irina Choukline.

Monica said, "I work for two different companies, MWHMC and AAA Hotel Service, and I have never met either of the bosses, and they were Anton Kim and Damir Brkanovich." Monica said Serguei was supposed to be the person who handles the area. There is another person by the name of Rick, but she did not know his last name. Rick deals with the people from the Czech Republic and she believed that this is a new company that Serguei is beginning in the area, and Serguei will be the "Representative" for that company in the area as well.

Monica said that someone from the Branson Postal Express called Serguei Choukline about a problem of not getting the mail. Serguei came to her home and took her to Starbucks for a coffee and then all of a sudden to the Branson Postal Express to change names on the mail box. Serguei was like that she said, he would just do things out of the blue. Even after a discussion with employees at the Branson Postal Express, she was still allowed to pick up the mail and would still give it all to Irina Choukline.

We asked her about the name of Irina Lemetyuynen who was supposed to be her boss with the title of Vice President of Human Services. Monica stated that she never knew this person and that she never worked at the hotel while she was dealing with the employees.

She told us as it related to another person by the name of Agnieska Koblenc, she came as a temporary worker under the H2B program. She [Agnieska], tried to apply for an extension and Serguei filed her paperwork. Monica stated that she believed that was the case, because Serguei would ask her for any letters that came relating to Koblenc. Monica said that if she got any company letters or paperwork, it all came from Serguei Choukline even though it had Anton Kim's name on it, and she knew that Serguei kept copies of everything.

Monica said that as it related to her own application, she used Serguei, not an attorney to complete the application. She added that she knew that Serguei was lying about the information on the application, but she didn't think it was important and she didn't think anyone would get hurt and Serguei never explained anything to her. She said that she never asked Serguei to be a citizen, she just wanted to stay in the United States in hopes she could be with her husband and child. She said this was the opportunity for them to get together, it wasn't done for the money.

Monica said that the European girls were open with their affection and would throw themselves at Serguei Choukline, but she never saw him with anyone. She did say, she knew that Serguei was married in the Slovak Republic to Martina Pirohova, which she had told us about in the first interview and reiterated the fact that she had been to their apartment in the Slovak Republic. She went on to say, that all of the company records were maintained at Serguei's house. This concluded or second interview of Monica and we believed she was being truthful with us.

Agnieska Koblenc, a citizen and national of Poland, who was petitioned by Serguei Choukline and MWHMC initially as an H2B Temporary Worker and was purported to be employed by him for a period of at least two years. Serguei then, petitioned for her as an L1A Intracompany Transferee/Manager for MWHMC, which was subsequently granted from August of 2004 until August of 2007. On March 20, 2005, Agnieska Koblenc, filed a petition to become a Lawful Permanent Resident (LPR), Alien in the United States. The same documentation that was used to support the application for the L1A, was used in the application for the LPR status. Since the first application was based on fraud and the same paperwork used for this application, then it too is based on fraud and a violation of federal law.

AUSA David Barnes, the prosecuting attorney in this investigation is intending on superseding the original indictment and adding Koblenc so we needed to find her current location. Through our investigation it was purported, that she had fled to Florida after Serguei's arrest. We identified an address for her near Ft. Myers, Florida and had sent a collateral request for the RAC Office in Fort Myers to verify that she does indeed reside at that address. We requested that no enforcement action be taken at this time, even though her status was obtained by fraud, and she was deportable, we had criminal charges pending.

If you recall, Monica told us in her first and second interview, and we also found evidence in Serguei's residence that he was married to another woman, Martina Pirohova in the Slovak Republic. Serguei is currently released on a $50,000.00 bond and even though he has to report to federal probation officers three times per week, we are expecting him to attempt to flee the United States to avoid any further prosecution. We, because of the information we have uncovered pertaining to the second marriage, sent a collateral lead to the foreign attaché office that covers that area, which happens to be in Vienna, Austria. In our request, we asked the officers to verify several things to include, Serguei's status in the Slovak Republic, the address that is believed to be Serguei and Martina's home address, if there is a marriage license in the Slovak Republic relating to their marriage there, to determine if there are any criminal allegations associated with Serguei in that country and to inform the officials of the fraud perpetrated by Serguei in the United States and the letter that he had directed Martina to file with the immigration official of the Slovak Republic.

Anticipating that the superseding indictment will add several other individuals to the indictment to include Agnieska Koblenc and will include additional charges, we began to determine the location of others such as Anya Bauer and Irina Lemetyuynen, as well as Serguei's wife Irina Choukline. We had already sent a collateral request to Ft. Myers, FL to verify the location of Agnieska Koblenc. We have since learned that she has returned to the area and was residing at an address in Branson, Missouri. We knew that Irina Choukline was still residing in Springfield, Missouri, and we know that Irina Lemetyuynen was also residing in Springfield, Missouri.

It was determined through our investigation and a collateral request for SAC Washington, D.C. that Anya Bauer is currently residing in Falls Church, Virginia and that she had resided at this location since about April 2005. It is unknown to us if Bauer knows of what has been happening in Springfield,

Missouri with the arrest of Serguei and Monica and whether or not she sees herself as a target. It was requested that SAC Washington not make contact with her and if a superseding indictment names Bauer, that they assist in the arrest operation.

In the meantime, as other phases of the investigation continue. Special Agent John Cress, with the United States Department of Labor, conducted an interview of Merica Simion, an Investigator with the Department's Wage and Hour Division relating to insufficient funds paid by MWHMC to its employees.

The interview indicated that from May of 2002 through September 2004, MWHMC underpaid 112 employees approximately $12,000.00. Simion told Cress that her main point of contact during her investigation was Anya Bauer who was identified as the Regional Director of Employee Management for MWHMC. Choukline introduced himself briefly and identified her point of contact as Anya Bauer. Simion told Cress, that she had inquired about the identity and location of the Vice President of MWHMC Anton Kim. She was told by both Choukline and Bauer that Kim was overseas or traveling on business. She went on to say that Bauer was responsible for payroll, human resources, and miscellaneous business duties associated with MWHMC. Bauer was also responsible for the distribution of payroll and collecting housing payments, as well as the day-to-day point of contact for MWHMC foreign labor and added that Bauer was knowledgeable of the foreign labor program. Simion did say that during her meetings with Bauer she seemed nervous and paranoid and when she spoke of Anton Kim, she became extremely nervous and fidgety.

Our investigation has led us down several paths in our attempts to come to the truth and identify not only the business operations of MWHMC but now AAA Hotel Services Inc, and possibly even another business that Serguei was about to start in conjunction with these two companies that we may have stopped. We, however, do not know the name of the third business that Monica Lopez-Rodriguez told us about in our interview. We were attempting to identify Anton Kim, but now we have Damir Brkanovich and a Ukrainian Passport found with Serguei's photograph on it in the name of Ruslan Semenchenko. Is this the name of the President or Vice President of the third company that might be J and J? Is this the company that was about to be started? Was Serguei going to be the "Point of Contact in the Area." Who knows but I think he may be running a little bit scared at this point in time and John and I, as well as AUSA Barnes are worried that he may be attempting to flee the United States.

If you remember, Serguei who we believed to have been afraid for his wife Irina and son and the potential for their arrest, fled to Russian near the end of our first investigation and was gone for a couple of years. He is now facing more charges, and looking at jail time here in the United States, what is his next move? He is unpredictable as Monica has alluded to. He has a wife in the Slovak Republic, he has a Slovak identity documents and status in the Slovak Republic, he has now what is believed to be a fake Ukrainian Passport in the name of Ruslan Semenchenko. We believe that he has plenty of places to go if he decided to flee and wouldn't have any worries. What is it that Monica said, "Serguei likes to play James Bond, he likes to do things on the spur of the moment, he likes to keep thing suspicious." Our decision was, he is going to flee, and we need to get him back in custody as soon as possible. Maybe after the next indictment we can justify to the court our belief and concerns and why.

On November 15, 2006, a Special Grand Jury was held for the United States District Court for the Western District of Missouri at Kansas City, Missouri and gave a True Bill, or approved a 17-count indictment adding to the Indictment the already charged Serguei Choukline and Monica Lopez-Rodriguez with new charges as follows:

Count One; 18 USC 371, All defendants, Conspiracy to Make False Statements and commit Mail Fraud, Visa Fraud and Alien Inducement; Counts Two and Five: 18 USC 1001, Serguei Choukline, Irina Choukline and Irina Lemetyuynen, False Statements; Counts Three and Six: 18 USC 1341, Serguei Choukline, Irina Choukline and Irina Lemetyuynen, Mail Fraud; Counts Four and Seven, Serguei Choukline, Irina Choukline and Irina Lemetyuynen, Visa Fraud; Counts Eight and Eleven, Serguei Choukline, Irina Choukline and Agnieszka Koblenc, 18 USC 1001 False Statements; Counts Nine and Twelve: Serguei Choukline, Irina Choukline and Agnieszka Koblenc, 18 USC 1341, Mail Fraud; Counts Ten and Thirteen: Serguei Choukline, Irina Choukline and Agnieszka Koblenc, 18 USC 1546, Visa Fraud; Counts Fourteen, Fifteen, and Sixteen: Serguei Choukline, 8 USC 1324, Inducement of Aliens to Remain in the United States: and Count Seventeen, Serguei Choukline and Irina Choukline, 18 USC 982, Forfeiture of Residence.

Based on the superseding indictment that has charged all of the other defendants in the investigation, Irina Choukline, Anya Bauer, Irina Lemetyuynen and Agnieska Koblenc, I had put forward an operation plan for the arrests of all of the defendants in this investigation in Springfield, Missouri, Branson, Missouri and Falls Church, Virginia. The Operations Plan was approved and all offices, Kansas City, Missouri, Springfield, Missouri and Washington, D.C. were onboard and ready to proceed. We can't forget, John Cress, and his agents from the United States Department of Labor who are a major part of this investigation.

On November 16, 2006, at 5:30 AM the arrest operation was initiated in all cities associated with this investigation. Agnieska Koblenc was arrested at her residence in Branson, Missouri without incident. What does without incident mean? It means that there were no altercations, no resistance on the part of the defendant, in other words, everything went smoothly, and no one was hurt in the process. Irina Lemetyuynen was arrested in the parking lot of her place of employment in Springfield, Missouri without incident. Anya Bauer was arrested at her place of residence in Falls Church, Virginia by agents from the SAC Washington, D.C. office. She too was arrested without incident. They were all turned over to the respective United States Marshal's Service in their areas to have their first appearances before the United States Magistrate. The last person to be arrested was Irina Choukline, Serguei's wife and the rearrest of Serguei to face the additional charges. John Cress and I attempted to execute arrest warrant on Irina and Serguei at their residence at 5:50 AM. We knocked at the door several times but there was no answer. We did not know if they were in the residence or not, so we could not go in without a warrant. We then went to Irina's place of work, the hospital where she was working as a Surgical Nurse, which we will talk about later. Her co-workers protected her. They would not give us any assistance in locating her at all. We even advised them that if it were determined that they were hiding a fugitive, now that they know we had a warrant for her arrest, they could be charged for aiding and abetting a fugitive from justice, but that didn't matter, there was still no assistance provided.

We kind of expected this, but our concerns as always is the possible flight to avoid prosecution. Serguei and Irina did not care for the other persons indicted with them, they did not care for any of the employees that were employed by them or by their company, all they cared for were themselves. Yes, Serguei has another wife, and has at least two additional identities. We were unable to determine if Irina had any such identities. She was now a United States citizen. Her intent was to live in and remain in the United States of America. After all, they had a United States citizen child who was now an adult and serving in the United States Marine Corps Reserves. He was an American war hero; he had already had a tour of duty in a war zone and saved a fellow soldiers' life. He was a hero in the eyes of the United States and his parents as he should be. Why would she want to depart the United States?

Later in the day, AUSA David Barnes, contacted the attorney for Serguei and Irina Choukline and arrangements were made for them, since there were additional charges brought on him, for them both to turn themselves in to the United States Marshal Service in Springfield, Missouri at 2:30

PM that afternoon. Monica Lopez-Rodriguez was allowed to remain out on bond.

At about 2:45 PM, they both appeared to our amazement, and turned themselves in. Serguei was already released on a $50,000.00 bond, but they both had their first appearance before the United States Magistrate as it related to the additional charges in the new indictment. Serguei was able to remain free on the original bond and Irina Choukline was released on a $25,000.00 bond. As it related to Irina Lemetyuynen and Agnieska Koblenc were held in custody pending a further detention hearing on December 1, 2006. An HSI detainer was filed on both Lemetyuynen and Koblenc. Bauer was released from the jurisdiction of Washington, D.C, and directed to report to the United States Marshal Service in Springfield, Missouri on November 22, 2006, for further court action.

AUSA David Barnes, based on these new charges, filed a Motion to reconsider the release conditions of Serguei Choukline due to our new evidence and concerns that he will flee from the United States to avoid prosecution. The hearing is scheduled for December 6, 2006.

Chapter Eight

Witness Intimidation

We have made our arrests based on the superseding indictment to include Serguei Choukline, his wife Irina Choukline, Monica Lopez-Rodriguez, Irina Lemetyuynen, Anya Bauer and Agnieska Koblenc. All are in custody or released on bond.

We did the same this time with the new arrests that we did with Serguei and with Monica Lopez-Rodriguez, we read them their appropriate Miranda Warning as required by law since they were now in custody and gave them the opportunity to answer questions about the offenses they are being charged with. Like Monica, they will be interviewed first and if they decide at a later date, they want to take a plea, they will be given the opportunity to give us a second interview or not. That is, at this point in the game, the decision of the AUSA's as to whether or not he wants to force them to give an interview of any kind, or accept the plea offered without it.

The interviews are important! Do we need them? Well, in a sense yes. We have the evidence, we know what happened, because we have the written documentation. We have the witnesses from all of the hotels, the mail drop boxes, businesses that have done business with MWHMC, and we have Serguei's own comments. The comments that he has made to the foreign labor force that have come forward. The workers that have decided to complain about the way they were brought to the United States, the way they were over charged for their travel or after arrival in the United States, the way they were paid while here, and the way they were physically treated during the time they were employed by him. The interview that puts his purported co-conspirators on the spot in that if they lie during the interview then the plea deal is off the table, and they go to trial. It is an incentive for them to get the best deal possible under the law. So, when the co-conspirators come forward and are willing to tell the truth about the events, it may clear up some suspicions and questions that we may have had. When we get the opportunity to conduct the interview, we have to sit down and review the evidence that is related to Serguei's relationship with that particular co-conspirator to know and have a better understanding of what occurred between them as it relates to the criminal offense that was committed in the visa fraud scheme. John and I did just that. When we received notification from any of the defendants that have come forward, we sat down and reviewed the evidence and determined the questions that needed to be asked and answered by this defendant. That was the case with Irina Lemetyuynen.

Lemetyuynen was arrested outside of her place of employment in Springfield, Missouri and due to the early hours of the arrests, we transported her to the HSI Office in Springfield, Missouri while we waited for the United States Marshal's Office to open. Lemetyuynen while waiting for transportation decided after being given her Miranda Warning, she wanted to speak to us, so John and I accepted her offer, we let her tell her side, and this is what she said:

She said that she last entered the United States in April 2002 as a Nonimmigrant B-1/B-2 Visitor for Business and Pleasure. She said that she owned her own travel agency called Irina Travel Company and had come to the United States to visit and travel. She stated that she had met Serguei Choukline on one of his visits to Moscow, Russia when he came to her travel business and introduced himself. Lemetyuynen said that she knew a friend of Serguei's by the name of Gregory Tempkin, who owns another travel agency. She said that Tempkin had entered the United States in about 1997. Lemetyuynen said that she and Serguei Choukline spoke about the travel business, and he told her that Gregory said hello and that was the extent of their first meeting and he left.

When she first entered the United States, she was in New York visiting Gregory Tempkin. Serguei found out that she was there and told her to come to Joplin, Missouri and she could go to work for his company. She said she came to Missouri and went to work for Serguei and his company. She said she never went to Joplin, but ended up working for his business in Springfield, Missouri. She said her responsibilities were to handle the payroll and didn't even work every day, and when she was needed for work, it was either Ann or Serguei who would call her when they needed her. She said her title at the company was Vice President, but she never did any Vice-Presidential duties, because Serguei really didn't want her to know what was going on in the company. Lemetyuynen said that Ann was a short, blonde haired younger girl, and there was another girl named "Ylena," but she believed she [Ylena], returned to Russia. Lemetyuynen continued saying that she only worked for Serguei for about two months, but she said when Serguei and his wife Irina came to work, they always arrived at work together.

Lemetyuynen was asked by John if she ever knew of Serguei using any other names? She hesitated to answer and asked if her family in Russia would be, okay? She was advised that we had no control over her family situation in Russia but would make her concerns known to the appropriate people. She then continued and said that it was Serguei Choukline's responsibility to sign all payroll checks, and she saw him sign them all in the name of Anton Kim. She went on to say that when she filed receipts in the receipt book that were given to her by Serguei from his various trips abroad all of the receipts were signed by "Anton Kim." She continued saying that she had been with Serguei and seen Serguei sign receipts with the name of Anton Kim. Lemetyuynen said she believed Serguei Choukline, and Anton Kim were the same person.

Lemetyuynen said that her application for her L1A Intracompany Transferee Temporary Worker visa was filed by Serguei Choukline, and she watched him sign it with the name of Anton Kim as well. She stated that she and Irina Choukline signed payroll checks in the name of Anton Kim. She stated that while she worked for Serguei, he kept all of her wages for himself for filing the L1A visa application, she said she believed he charged her $6,000.00 to file the application on her behalf.

Lemetyuynen said that her ex-husband owned a company called Griol in Russia. She said that the information that was provided on her application using the company name of Griol was all made up. Serguei Choukline had no business relationship with Griol whatsoever!

Serguei Choukline signed her application in the name of Anton Kim and then gave the application to her to sign. He then told her that she needed to send the application and Serguei kept copies of the entire application in his office and told her to keep her mouth shut about the application or he would send her to jail and have her deported.

She continued saying that she did not know anyone by the name of Monica Lopez. She said in August of 2006, she received a telephone call from an unknown male caller who told her she needed to leave Springfield, Missouri. The caller went on to tell her that if she talked to anyone about MWHMC that her parents in Russia and her family in the United States would have problems. She then said, a few weeks later, after she pulled into the parking lot of the United States Post Office in Springfield, Missouri, Serguei pulled into the parking space adjacent to her. Serguei asked her why she wouldn't speak to him, and she said she told him about the telephone call, and she did not know the voice. He told her "Don't worry, I will find out about it." Serguei then asked her if anyone called her about her work at MWHMC to which she told him "No!" She said that she believed that it was too much of a coincidence that he arrived at the same time that she did and believed that Serguei had followed her to the Post Office. She said she had moved to another address and did not tell Serguei and Irina where she had moved to and didn't know how he found her. The interview was terminated, and she was transported to the United States District Court in Springfield for her first appearance.

Now that Serguei's wife, Irina Choukline was included in the indictment and had been charged with the conspiracy to commit visa fraud as well as other charges, I began to look back at any complaints or allegations against her. I found that during the in-between case period in December of 2001, a person by the name of Kira Stogsdale, came to the then INS Office, Springfield, Missouri. Stogsdale said that she witnessed her mother pay Serguei Choukline $3,000.00 for a nursing license from Russia. Stogsdale stated that this is a license that Serguei personally produced for her mother. Stogsdale stated that her mother had never attended the Severodvinsk Medical University and never obtained a nursing degree status. Stogsdale stated that Serguei's wife Irina Choukline was able to obtain her job as a nurse at the hospital in Springfield, Missouri by presenting the same type of diploma to the State of Missouri. Stogsdale went on to say that Irina Choukline studied at home for two years to learn enough to pass her test but had never practiced or studied nursing prior to coming to the United States. Wow, that was quite a statement, especially about someone who had been a nurse at the local hospital for a long time. This was certainly out of my prevue as an investigator, and I would have to contact the State of Missouri to find out to whom this type of complaint would have to be given. If this is true, and I do say if, this is dangerous and could open the hospital to all kinds of law suits.

Serguei Choukline and his wife Irina as well as Monica are out on bond, but everyone else is still in custody because of their Immigration Status and a detainer filed with the Marshal's Service. But like I have said over and over, the investigation doesn't stop at this point. We have witnesses to identify and determine who will be called and who will not be called to testify. The development of witnesses is challenging to say the least. We too looked at all of the statements and interviews that we have conducted over the last couple of years during this investigation and determine if the information a particular person provided was enough to constitute them as a witness to testify in a court proceeding against Serguei and the rest of those indicted. So now, all of the mundane work as many would say, going through all of the material, comparing it to evidence, to paperwork and applications, bank accounts, names on applications and bank accounts, contractual agreements etc. comparing everything to each other and to the statements that we have received from other defendants as well.

On November 20, 2006, while sitting in my office, going over notes and interviews, etc., I received a telephone call from Robert Ogrodnik, Honorary Counsel for the Polish Consulate in St. Louis, Missouri as it related to Agnieska Koblenc, a citizen and national of Poland and her detention status. I informed Ogrodnik that Ms. Koblenc was currently in the custody of the United States Marshal Service in Springfield, Missouri based on the indictment and arrest. Ogrodnik then asked if this had anything to do with an individual in Springfield, Missouri by the name of Serguei Choukline. I found this kind of awkward initially, that he would be asking about Serguei but then I thought since, Serguei hired foreign labor from all over the world, maybe the Polish government had received some complaints or had information that would be beneficial to our investigation. I informed Mr. Ogrodnik that it did. Ogrodnik stated that he had met Serguei Choukline at one time relating to a previous matter pertain to Polish citizens that worked for him [Serguei], not being paid. Ogrodnik stated that he and Serguei had went to lunch together to discuss the matter and he found it funny that Serguei would tell him out of the blue that he was ex-KGB, Russian Secret Service. Ogrodnik stated that he was taken aback by this information, but then said he didn't have any further information as it related to Serguei's claims, but he then said, "If Choukline is ex-KGB, he was indeed a dangerous individual." Our telephone call was concluded at this time.

Then as time went on that afternoon, I remember during my first investigation when my ADDI told us, and especially me because of my investigation, that a person of Russian descent that was under investigation in and around the Seattle, Washington area had appeared at the door of the INS agent conducting an investigation against them. Lastly, the confrontation of Serguei and Irina Lemetyuynen at the Post Office. Was Ogrodnik a real consular officer or was this one of Serguei's friends trying to intimidate like he has in the past or am I getting a little paranoid. I am not paranoid; I am not worried about Serguei and believe that Serguei will get his just due in time. However, the information was passed on to the AUSA David Barnes. I did later look up Robert Ogrodnik and a person by that name is indeed a Polish Consular Officer based in St. Louis, Missouri.

On November 28, 2006, I did contact Supervisory Investigator Quinn Lewis, of the Missouri State Board of Nursing in Jefferson City, Missouri. This is the agency within the State of Missouri that investigates any allegations against anyone in the medical field that has a license to work in this state. I passed on the information that I had received from Kira Stogsdale. Lewis was only able to give me a little bit of information but said that Irina Choukline's nursing license was transferred from the State of Alaska, and she had provided a certificate from the Severodvinsk Medical University in Severodvinsk, Russia. Does that sound familiar? Kira said that her mother paid Serguei $3,000.00 to provide her a fictitious medical certificate from this hospital in Russia. Well, the information is in the hands of the correct agency to conduct the proper investigation and that part of it is out of my hands.

On December 6, 2006, the court ruled once again in Serguei's favor, even after testimony and the presentation of evidence that he was a flight risk and allowed him to remain out on bond.

On December 14, 2006, the United States District Court ruled in favor of Agnieska Koblenc and released her on bond pending any further hearings or trials. Because I had placed a detainer with the Marshal Service, Koblenc was returned to the Greene County Jail, but this time under the jurisdiction of ICE/DR (Immigration and Customs Enforcement, Detention and Removal). On December 15, 2006, officers from ICE picked up Koblenc and transported her to HSI Springfield, Missouri for processing and to be placed in removal proceedings for visa fraud. Prior to serving the Notice to Appear on Koblenc, I received a call from her attorney in the criminal case. The attorney, I'll just call Stacy, said that she had received a call from Koblenc's husband stating that we were on our way to

"Interrogate" Koblenc as it relates to the criminal case and that she had contacted another immigration attorney to see if this is true. I told her that was not the intent, that the encounter with Koblenc was to do nothing but serve her the Notice to Appear advising her of the Immigration allegations against her. Stacy told me that she didn't think that would be the case but had to protect her client and wanted to confirm what she had been told.

On December 15, 2006, I met with Agnieska Koblenc at the HSI Office in Springfield, Missouri to serve the Notice to Appear (NTA), the administrative charging document. Koblenc was told that this was not a criminal allegation that it was strictly administrative charges dealing with her own visa fraud allegations. I also told her that because she was being charged in a criminal case, the Miranda Rights that were provided to her previously still applied and she would not be asked any questions that might incriminate her in any way as it relates to her criminal case. Koblenc said that she understood.

I then served the NTA, the Administrative Warrant and Bond Form, which indicated Koblenc was going to be held without bond. After I finished serving her the NTA, Koblenc was asked if she had any questions before I left and Koblenc said she did want to ask some questions and asked the following.

She asked how her criminal case would affect her administrative case.

I told her that it all depended on the outcome of the criminal case. I went on to say that if she were convicted of any of the charges that made her an aggravated felon, that this would probably mean some jail time and her NTA would be changed to include the aggravated felony charge. If she was deported as an aggravated felon, this is a 20-year ban from the United States unless she obtained permission from the Attorney General of the United States to reapply to enter the United States.

She looked and me and said she wanted to cooperate with the government!

To this I told her that the government had already made an offer for a plea to her attorney and if she and her attorney decided to accept that offer then the government would make arrangements to conduct another interview of her as it relates to the criminal case. I told her she would then plea to the agreed upon charge that she and her attorney decided on, and she would then be able to testify against Serguei Choukline. If she too declined the plea offer, then we would go to trial. She was told that here in the United States, she has the right to have a trial to face her accusers, in this case, the government. I also told her, that she has the right to hear all of the evidence against her and she and her attorney can contest the evidence, cross examine the witnesses and hope the jury rules in their favor. If she did not plea, then her attorney may not want her to testify. I told her that the United States government felt they have a good case against her, or it would not have been presented for prosecution. On the other hand, her defense attorney felt that they have a good case and can defeat the allegations as well. The outcome of the trial would determine if any further administrative allegations would be brought against her or not.

Koblenc said she believed she was offered the opportunity to plea to all of the allegations identified in the indictment.

I told her again that she might want to contact her attorney as she may have misunderstood the plea offer made to her by the government. Unless there was conversation other than what I was present for, the offer was for her to plea to one count of a violation of 18 USC 1001, False Statements, which is not a deportable offense in most cases. She was again told that she needed to contact her attorney to discuss any offers made by the government to make sure she thoroughly understood the offer.

Koblenc then asked if she accepted the offer of the government, would she be released from jail.

I told her that her attorney could ask the government to put in the plea agreement that the government would request that ICE reconsider her bond conditions. She was also told if she accepted the offer of the government and settled her case that would likely alleviate some of the concerns of ICE as it relates to her being a flight risk and could weigh in her favor on the bond/detention issues.

She then asked about the court process and stated that she wanted to testify against Choukline as he had destroyed her, and she was in jail, and he was out on bond.

I then told her that Choukline was a resident alien in the United States and was not subject to deportation unless he was convicted of a crime that would make him deportable. Koblenc on the other hand, the government felt there was sufficient evidence to prove that she obtained her status by fraud. By obtaining her status by fraud subjects her not only to criminal charges but administrative charges as well and this is why the detainer was placed against her. As far as the court process, The United States Attorney and agents set at one table, the defendants and their attorneys set at another table. The attorneys present their case and their witnesses to the court and to the jury, and they determine guilt or innocence. If the jury decides she is guilty then sentencing guidelines will determine if she goes to jail or not and for how long. If she is found innocent, then she will still have to face the administrative charges that were filed against her in the NTA served today.

She then asked me about the sentencing guidelines and that she didn't understand.

I then asked her if she remembered the indictment, the charges identified a maximum number of years that she could be sentenced to and in her case, it was about 30 years. She became a little upset I told her to calm down and relax that there had to be a maximum number of years available for criminals who were repeat offenders. By having a range of time that could be imposed on a criminal, the criminal for the first offense could be given a small amount of jail time or none at all, but as they continue to commit crimes then a longer sentence could be imposed based on their continued criminal activity. She was told if she had no other criminal history that would be taken into consideration by the people who made those decisions on how much time she could be sentenced.

Her big question was if she would have to sit next to or near Choukline in the trial process.

I told her that would depend on the way the trial is handled, but that was a possibility. She once again became upset and stated she didn't want to be near him at all.

She then asked me if she accepted the governments offer, would this charge be added to her administrative charging document.

I told her again that she had the right to have a trial and face her accusers, but after she spoke again with her husband and attorney and if she decided she wanted to accept the governments offer, if it were still the offer of a plea to one count of false statements, that this was not normally a deportable offense and may or may not be added to the immigration document.

She was truly concerned about her deportation, as I would be, and asked if this would affect her deportation.

I told her that it would still be a conviction in her file, but possibly not a deportable conviction. With the government's offer to inform Immigration Attorneys of her cooperation in a criminal case and how her assistance helped in that investigation, it was thought that it would certainly be taken into consideration at the time of her deportation hearing. I told her again that she had an attorney in the criminal case and should confide in her as it relates to considering any plea offers or agreements with the government that she might be considering.

She asked if I thought this would be the best thing for her.

I told her once again, that she had an attorney and should have that conversation with her attorney and that it was not my place to have that discussion with her. She was again told she really needed to speak to her attorney relating to those types of questions.

I then, upon completing service of the NTA to Koblenc, told her of the telephone conversation with Stacy, her attorney, who was concerned that I was going to interrogate her pertaining to her criminal case. She then said that she had told her husband Jason Arredondo that I was coming to speak to her but did not say anything about an interrogation. She said she appreciated that I had told her this information. She then said or confirmed that she was not asked any questions regarding her criminal case and that I had only answered her questions.

I didn't want to take any chances of being accused of asking her any questions relating to her criminal case, so I made sure this entire conversation took place in the presence of a Supervisory Immigration Enforcement Agent and an Immigration Enforcement Agent as witnesses.

There were no further discussions at this time with Koblenc. The information that we discussed during this meeting was immediately passed on to AUSA David Barnes to ensure that everything that was talked about was disclosed.

Things are beginning to come together. The minions of Serguei, or I should say those that he seemed to lure into his lair were beginning to turn on him. Even though they were facing criminal charges themselves as well as possible jail time and future deportation, it was better than living a life indebted to Serguei and the consequences of his threats to them and their family both in the United States and abroad.

On February 13, 2007, John Cress and I met at the United States District Courthouse for the Western District of Missouri, Southern Division at Springfield, Missouri for the purpose of conducting an interview of Irina Lemetyuynen and her attorney along with a Russian Interpreter.

Lemetyuynen told us that she met Serguei in about 2000 or 2001 while still in Russia as she had told us before, she owned her own travel agency and Serguei showed up and said that they had a mutual friend Gregory Tempkin and Serguei introduced himself and said that Gregory said hello. She repeated that Gregory Tempkin also owned and operated a Travel Agency in Russia and she had met him at a conference, and they use to call one another for assistance.

Lemetyuynen, said that she wanted to provide some background information relating to the period of time that she was still residing in Russia. She said that her ex-husband was one of three owners of Griol that she had mentioned earlier. Griol was a construction business. She went on to say that the other two owners in 1992, backed out of the business leaving her husband as the sole owner. During the existence of Griol, Choukline and or MWHMC were never associated with or employed by Griol in any way. She said that Serguei supposedly did own a business in Russia, but she did not know what it was. She continued on repeating the same information that she had provided in her initial interview of how she arrived in New York and stayed with Tempkin, how she came to work with Serguei in Springfield, Missouri and how Serguei used the information of her ex-husbands company of Griol to apply for her to receive a visa in the United States. Lemetyuynen did state that they used a law firm in New York to apply for the visa and that after it was completed and signed by them, she mailed it to the law firm who forwarded it to the appropriate service center. Lemetyuynen said that all of the Griol letterhead that was sent as a part of the application was fraudulent, as well as all of the documents and statements. Serguei told her that it cost him $17,000.00 for his visa so that was what it was going to cost her, and she paid him in increments.

Lemetyuynen said that she started working for Serguei at his Springfield office in about 2004 and as Serguei took her around to the other tenants in the building introducing her, he introduced her as one of his employees who had been out on maternity leave which was untrue. Serguei told her one time as she worked on payroll if the federal government came into the office and asked any questions about the business, don't be afraid, it was okay. He also told her if anyone had any questions about the payroll to contact Monica. She said that she also worked with Anya Bauer and one day she saw her working on the payroll which is what she was supposed to do and when she confronted her about it, Bauer told her it was none of her business and told her payroll was not her responsibility. Lemetyuynen stated that she believed that Serguei and Bauer were involved in a relationship.

Lemetyuynen told us that she kept seeing business documents in the name of Anton Kim and saw Serguei and Irina signing payroll checks in the name of Anton Kim, she stated that when Serguei was out of town, she would go to his house and give the information to Irina. One day, after about a month and a half, she asked Irina and Anya why everyone signed Anton

Kim on MWHMC paperwork. They tried to tell her that she had met him in the past at a conference. Lemetyuynen stated that she has never met Anton Kim and based on her dealings with the business she believes that Anton Kim does not exist and the Choukline's are forging his name.

She went on to say that in the summer of 2005, Serguei came to her house inquiring if she had received her green card yet or not and she advised that she had not. He told her that she would probably have an interview with immigration and began to coach her on how to answer questions and instructed her what to say if asked about MWHMC and that neither he nor his wife worked at MWHMC any longer, that they only shared office space with MWHMC.

She said in about January of 2005, Serguei again met her at her residence and was asking questions about whether or not she had received her resident alien card. She said by this time she had received it but did not want to pay Serguei the money she owed him, so she told him she had not. Lemetyuynen said it was interesting, because she asked Serguei one time why his wife and son had citizenship and he did not. She was told by Serguei, "I don't want to be a United States citizen, because I am a citizen of Slovakia and Russia. I only want the United States money, that I can send to Slovakia and Russia."

She went on to say that in late January of 2006, Irina Choukline called her and requested that she come to her home. She stated that she went to the Choukline's residence in Springfield, Missouri where she met Irina. Irina directed her to the backyard and advised that she did not want to talk inside their home because federal authorities had just been there. Irina informed Lemetyuynen that Serguei and Monica had been arrested and told her that she would be the next to be arrested because of her association with MWHMC. Irina went on to tell her that all of her immigration documents were supported by MWHMC and because she was the Vice President of MWHMC, and she was responsible for the companies' activities. Irina reiterated that she and Serguei never worked for MWHMC and if the federal authorities ever ask her about Anton Kim, she needed to explain to them that Anton Kim hired her. She said she then asked, "Who is Anton Kim?" Irina responded: "Anton Kim was a student worker who was here before you [Lemetyuynen] came to the United States." Irina Choukline then requested that Irina Lemetyuynen drive her to the nearest convenience store so she could call Gregory Tempkin to inform him about Serguei's arrest. After the telephone call, Irina instructed her not to contact the authorities and to leave the Springfield, Missouri area because of her association with MWHMC.

Lemetyuynen said that a couple of weeks later, she got a phone call from Gregory Tempkin on behalf of Serguei and he asked if anyone had contacted her to which she replied they had not. Tempkin then instructed her to leave Springfield and not to cooperate with the authorities. He then reiterated the fact that Lemetyuynen was the Vice President of MWHMC and that she was responsible for the actions of the company.

On an unknown date in August of 2006, she received a telephone call from a male caller who identified himself as Anton Kim. She said the call came from an unknown telephone number and from a male caller who she did not recognize the voice. She said the person on the other end of the line tried to convince her that he was Anton Kim, and that they had met in the past and that she knew who he was. Evidently, whoever called her did not know about the conversation that she had with Serguei's wife, Irina when she finally identified who Anton Kim was, a student who worked for MWHMC before she came. She stated she hung up the phone. She said later in the same week, she received a phone call from an unknown Russian male who told her to leave Springfield, and not to talk to anyone about MWHMC or her family in Russia and in the United States would have problems.

She then spoke of her encounter with Serguei in the parking lot of the Post Office in Springfield and was told the same story. Lemetyuynen then told us that she had found out some information about Serguei while he was in Russia that he used to be the deputy mayor in Vologda and that he had murdered someone for an accident involving his car, and that he was able to pay the Russian authorities to dismiss his murder charges.

This concluded our interview of Lemetyuynen, and the dominoes are continuing to fall. The stories that we were getting from everyone was the same. Serguei and Irina didn't work for MWHMC, naming the other defendants as corporate officers so they could be blamed for everything, and no one knows who the anonymous Anton Kim was. But, thanks to statements made by Irina Choukline and Lemetyuynen willingness to testify in court, we now know!

On August 29, 2007, due the earnings that Serguei and Irina had made through their criminal visa fraud scheme, a Lis Pendens was levied against their home with the Recorder of Deeds in Greene County Springfield, Missouri which basically stops the home from being sold on a quitclaims deed to s family member or friend to avoid being seized by the government.

In September 2007, I received a somewhat frantic call from Monica Lopez-Rodriguez. Monica is a co-defendant in this investigation, but she has given us an interview and is willing to plea to a lesser charge. She is out on bond and is living at her home in Branson, Missouri with her mother and brother, who if you remember was released from ICE custody after being administratively charged so they could care for Monica's three-year old child while she was in custody. Monica was advised that if she had any problems during her release with threats from Serguei's family or anyone else, she could call. Well, she did just that.

Monica called me and told me that she had received a document in the mail, which appeared to be some type of letter stating all kinds of lies against her, her mother, brother, and her husband who is now in Russia. The letter told her that she could withdraw her plea agreement in this case and then she could return to Mexico on her own without any further charges.

Monica was asked to fax the document to me at my office in Kansas City. I told her after she faxed it, to put the document carefully in a plastic bag, put it in an envelope and mail it to my office in Kansas City, Missouri. She did as she was instructed, she faxed the letter to me that very day and mailed it as well. As

I reviewed the information it appeared that it was some type of written report of investigation and ended just by saying "good luck" and was signed only by "J." The report or document had a lot of information that was blacked out, but in the title section of the document, it identified all of the defendants listed in the indictment. Of course, the names on the indictment and charges were identified in the press release given by the United States Attorney's Office after the arrests were made.

As I read the report, it accused Monica and her husband of being involved in drug trafficking, and that her child was present during the sale of narcotics. The letter also stated that her mother and brother should be investigated as well. The document went on to say that under Rule 12(d)(2), of the Rules of Criminal Procedures, she could withdraw her plea and depart the United States and "flea" (as in the bug that is a pest to your pet, not the flee, as in running away) and that she could not be extradited back to the United States, which is not true. There was also a statement in the report that said Monica was having an affair or sexual relationship with a person known as "Khorkhe." Monica, when we discussed this information on the telephone, told me that she had dated an individual known as "Jorge." She went on to say that she had told Serguei of this person's and Serguei could never pronounce his name properly and always called him "Corky." She had to continuously correct him in his pronunciation of the name, but he could never get it right. It was therefore believed by Monica that Serguei wrote the document and sent it to her in an attempt to get her to leave the United States and not testify against him.

Later in the month of September I received another call from Monica stating that her mother had now received a letter, and when she opened it, it was the exact same document and this time, the letter did not have a post mark on it. It appeared that it was just placed in her mail box and did not go through the postal system. I told her to put the document and the envelope in a plastic bag, put it in an envelope and mail it to me and it would be recovered as evidence.

Due to the receipt of these letters by Monica and the confrontation of Lemetyuynen with Serguei at the Post Office in the parking lot, AUSA David Barnes filed a motion in the United States District Court for the Southern District of Missouri in Springfield, Missouri to revoke the bond of Serguei and have him remanded to the custody of the United States Marshal Service pending the upcoming trial. We had a hearing to which I testified to the evidence we had against Serguei once again, as well as the threats against the other defendants. Serguei's attorney defended him by saying that Serguei and Irina were divorced, and he married Martina Pirohova and was living with Irina when in the United States for their son. The attorney went on to argue that Serguei has since divorced Martina Pirohova in the Republic of Slovakia and has remarried Irina and they have reconciled their marriage. The judge said he would rule at a later date, which he ruled in Serguei's favor and allowed him once again to remain out on bond. Unbelievable!

Since the judge did not remand Serguei back into the custody of the United States Marshal Service, Monica, her mother, her brother, and her three-year-old child were brought to Kansas City, Missouri and put in a hotel in protective custody until the trial. They would after the trial be returned to Branson, Missouri.

The next day, the two documents received from Monica were placed in evidence and sent to the ICE Forensics Document Lab in McLean, VA to determine if there were any other fingerprints on the documents other than probably those of Monica and her mother. A few days later, I received information from the Forensics Document Lab. The lab tech advised that there was a fingerprint found on the first document, but nothing on the second document. The fingerprint did not match that of Serguei, and it appeared to be a female print. Copies of fingerprints of Monica and Irina Choukline were sent to the lab and the only print found belonged to Monica Lopez-Rodriguez. Whoever produced this document knew very well how to cover their prints. Something that someone who had served in the intelligence field or KGB would have been trained to think of to do!

On October 3, 2007, we were given the opportunity to interview Agnieska Koblenc. John and I met with the United States attorneys David Barnes and Bruce Clark at the United States Attorney's Office in Springfield, Missouri along with Agnieska Koblenc and her attorney for a second interview. All of the appropriate paperwork was signed by the attorney and Agnieska and we began our interview.

Agnieska said that in about June of 2003 she became aware of a student exchange program that would allow her to travel abroad and enhance her education and experience in the restaurant industry. She said that Megotch, a travel company, offered her a one-and-a-half-year job offer in Florida and a seven-month job offer in Branson, Missouri. Koblenc said that she believed having this experience in the United States, would benefit her regarding potential employment in the restaurant industry in Europe. She said that she was informed by Megotch she had received an H2B Temporary Worker visa, sponsored by Anton Kim who represented MWHMC in Branson, Missouri. Koblenc said that she was responsible for logistics and travel finances which totaled about $2,000.00.

Koblenc said that she originally flew from Poland to Chicago, IL and then rented a vehicle with other students who drove to Branson, Missouri. She said that the instructions provided by MWHMC advised that the students go to the All-Seasons Hotel in Branson, Missouri and contact a female identified as Monica Lopez, but when they arrived at the hotel, Monica was not there. She said that she and the others waited in the hotel parking lot for the MWHMC representative to arrive and while they were waiting they met with other MWHMC students. She was told that they had been there about a week and were still waiting for employment. Later that evening, Monica arrived and instructed them to check into the hotel. She said once checked in, she learned that she would be rooming with three additional people and was responsible for the room rent. She said that Monica's husband Andre, was responsible for MWHMC student transportation.

She continued by telling us in this interview, that during this same week, Anya Bauer and Monica Lopez conducted interviews with the students to determine their education and job placement. Several of the students complained that they had been in Branson for several weeks and still didn't have employment. Koblenc said that she and several of the other students requested to meet Anton Kim because of not having work, and they were told by both Bauer and Lopez that Anton Kim was traveling on business and was not available.

She said she later in the same week met a white male by the name of Serguei Choukline who she recognized as sending her emails during her H2B application process. Serguei identified himself to the students as the manager of MWHMC. Serguei told them that their visas were issued in May and since they didn't arrive until June, they had to wait for their employment. She said everyone was upset and Serguei attempted to calm them all down by telling them that jobs will become available and to be patient. She said that she went on several interviews for a housekeeping position, but she really wanted to work in the restaurant industry. It was about two weeks later she was employed by The Hacienda and was working seventy to eighty hours per week. She said that after about a month of working these kinds of hours, she and the other employees were still not paid. She said that she explained the situation to Monica, Anya and Serguei, and again requested to speak to Anton Kim and was told by Serguei that he would be in Branson, Missouri in the near future. Koblenc said that she told Serguei that she was supposed to be paid overtime and was informed by Serguei that since they were Temporary Workers, they were not eligible for overtime. She said Anton Kim never came to Branson.

She said that she was however, approached later by Serguei in regard to the overtime that was due her. Serguei provided her with a receipt for the overtime payment and instructed her to sign the document and she observed that a check was attached to the document. She said that she was unable to see the amount on the check, but Serguei never provided her with the check, and she was told by Serguei to tell the authorities that she was paid her overtime, or she would lose her job at the Hacienda. She was later told by other students that Serguei provided them with the same type of document and advised them to tell the authorities the same thing or they too would lose their jobs.

Koblenc told us that after working for MWHMC for several months she and her boyfriend moved into their own apartment and was later approached by Serguei telling them that their visa was due to expire, and they had to pay him several hundred dollars to extend their visa and that they could remain working during this process. She said during this time, their paychecks were continuously late. Serguei told her that The Hacienda sent the checks in late, but when she approached The Hacienda about the late payments, they denied it and stated that they have paid MWHMC on time for all hours worked and that she should call MWHMC regarding back pay.

She said that when she did receive her paychecks, they were always signed by Anton Kim, but she had never met Anton Kim and the checks were delivered by either Monica or Anya. Monica told them after so many complaints, that they would have to come to the office in Springfield, Missouri to pick up their paychecks. She stated that after a while she saw that the company name changed from MWHMC to AAA Hotel Service Incorporated but was never notified of the company name change. Serguei told her that it was the same company, just a different name.

She continued with the fact that after her visa was extended, she was offered a supervisor's position with The Hacienda but was told she would have to negotiate her salary with MWHMC and that any pay increases would have to be authorized by Serguei Choukline. The Hacienda agreed to pay her more through Serguei for the promotion.

She said about the time of the end of the second extension of the H2B visas, Serguei held another meeting and offered to apply for her to get an L1A visa. She said she told Serguei that she was not an executive, but Serguei told her that she was a supervisor at The Hacienda, and through her position there, that would constitute her receiving an L1A visa. She said that Serguei charged her $6,000.00 to file the L1A visa application. She said she later became aware that the application and supporting documents contained numerous fictitious documents and that the application was signed by Anton Kim.

Koblenc said that Serguei appeared to be the person in charge of both MWHMC and AAA Hotel Services Inc. Monica and Anya handled all of the employee issues, because Serguei was always traveling overseas. When she asks Serguei about Anton Kim and who he is, Serguei is constantly attempting to convince her that she had met him in the past, but she has not and believes that Serguei Choukline and Anton Kim are one in the same person. Everything was signed by Anton Kim, but he was never around.

She continued and said that in February of 2006, she received an anonymous email, which advised that all MWHMC Hotel Managers had been arrested and the business has been closed. The email informed her and the other student to relocate as soon as possible so they would not be subject to deportation. She said that she believed that Serguei wrote this email, because she only provided her personal email address to a select number of individuals which included Serguei. She added that MWHMC/AAA Hotel Services did not pay her or the other students for their last month of work based on the aforementioned situation and added that she was hired directly by The Hacienda due to this situation. She added that she is willing to cooperate with this investigation.

We attempted to interview Anya Bauer and as we did, it was pretty much the same information as was given by everyone else as it relates to driving the workers around, helping them get to their hotels, work and back. It was all the same old information. What I remember the most is that she too was threatened. Serguei called her family in Russia and they in turn called Anya. They were not only afraid for themselves, but for Anya here in the United States.

Irina Choukline too agreed to plea to a lesser charge, but she would not provide an interview. We attempted a couple of times to contact her through her attorney, but she would not talk to us.

When it came to the plea agreement of Serguei, we wanted him to have to admit that he was Anton Kim, Damir Brkanovich and Ruslan Semenchenko. When Serguei's defense attorneys came to the United States Attorney's Office, the Wednesday before the trial was to officially begin on the following Monday, to review the evidence, David instructed John and I to stand outside the room when the attorney's reviewed our evidence. As a part of trial prep, they have the right to look at the evidence. Our evidence was mostly documentary other than witness testimony and consisted of eight of the long bankers document boxes, which contained all of the visa applications that were filed through not only the States of Missouri, but the Department of Labor and the Department of Homeland Security, Citizenship, and Immigration Services. I will admit, there was a lot of paper in those boxes. The attorney's had the right to review but could not remove anything from the room. After they reviewed the information for a couple of hours they departed and told David and Bruce they would speak to their client and get back in touch with them.

That was a very long few hours and it was getting into the evening, and they had not called or come back to the office, so we just thought it was a done deal, and we were going to trial next week. Then it came, the telephone call to come and meet with David and Bruce. They returned to the United States Attorney's Office in Springfield where we were in full trial preparation. They arrived and wanted to speak in a separate room but did not want John and I present during the discussion. I will tell you, that John and I were peeved to say the least. There were a few words of disgust exchanged between us and David and Bruce. Nothing vulgar, I am not saying that, but we were ticked that his defense attorneys could direct or expect us to stay out of the discussions of a plea agreement. John and I, though thoroughly distressed about this, conceded, and agreed to stay out of the discussion. After a couple of hours, David and Bruce came out of the meeting and informed us of what was discussed and what they tentatively agreed to but needed our concurrence. Serguei would plea to the one count of conspiracy to commit the visa fraud and the number of applications filed, not the number of visas applied for.

The sentencing guideline for this plea is substantially less than if he had pleaded guilty to the number of visas actually applied for. He would still be going to prison, but not near the amount of time he would get in the other case. He would stand and admit to the visa fraud but would not admit that he was Anton Kim, Damir Brkanovich or Ruslan Semenchenko. This upset John and I pretty good, because this was a major factor in the whole fraud scam. However, in any case, a plea agreement is better than nothing at all. What is the old saying "A bird in the hand is better than two in the bush." He was willing to admit his guilt and go to prison for it, as well as accept the judicial order of deportation. We all agreed with no regret to accept the plea that was offered. As you know Serguei was subsequently sent to prison, served his time, and was deported from the United States. No cost for a trial and paying forty plus witnesses to appear, and no long days in a court setting listening to all of the lies I am sure that we would have heard from the defense counsel on behalf of their client trying to discredit our witnesses. Let it go. Which we did.

After all of the interviews, were conducted, and plea agreements were made, the plea dates were set.

Chapter Nine

Pleas, Sentencings, and Serguei Still Not Giving Up

The plea dates were set for each of the defendants and John, and I travelled to Springfield Missouri for each one of them along with AUSA David Barnes.

On October 4, 2007, based on the plea agreement, Agnieska Koblenc pleaded guilty in the Western District of Missouri, Southern Division, at Springfield, Missouri to one count of a violation of Title 8, USC, Section 1306(c), knowingly make a false statement on an application for registration, a misdemeanor. Sentencing will be scheduled at a later date.

On the same date, Irina Lemetyuynen, based on the plea agreement, pleaded guilty in the Western District of Missouri, Southern Division, at Springfield, Missouri to one count of a violation of Title 8, USC, Section 1306(c), knowingly make a false statement on an application for registration, a misdemeanor. Sentencing will be scheduled at a later date.

On October 18, 2007, based on the plea agreement, Anya Bauer, pleaded guilty in the United States District Court for the Western District of Missouri, Southern Division at Springfield, Missouri to a single count of a violation of Title 18, USC, Section

4, and admitted to United States Magistrate Judge England, that she knew that false statements and misrepresentations were being provided on documentation associated with a federal violation, a felony and failed to report the offense to law enforcement. Sentencing will be scheduled at a later date.

On October 19, 2007, based on the plea agreement, Irina Choukline pleaded guilty in the Western District of Missouri, Southern Division, at Springfield, Missouri to one count of a violation of Title 8, USC, Section 1306(c), Irina Choukline admitted to United States Magistrate Judge England, that she was the Secretary for the company known as MWHMC, and that she knowingly made a false statement on an application for alien registration, a misdemeanor. Sentencing will be scheduled at a later date.

Lastly, on October 19, 2007, based on a plea agreement, Serguei D. Choukline pleaded guilty in the United States District Court for the Western District of Missouri, Southern Division, at Springfield, Missouri to a single count, charging a violation of Title 18, USC, 371, Conspiracy to commit 18, USC 1546, Visa Fraud. Serguei Choukline admitted to United States Magistrate Judge England, that he conspired with others to commit visas fraud by filing eighteen visa applications totaling over 300 visas by making false and fraudulent statements in the visa applications, a felony. Choukline is to surrender his bond and turn himself into the United States Marshal Service, Springfield, Missouri on October 22, 2007, at 3:00 PM. Sentencing will be scheduled at a later date.

The sentencings of the six defendants in this investigation would happen soon. This is the slow part it seems like as we wait for the dates to come, but we know that we are now moving into the final phase and toward the end of the investigation. Monica Lopez-Rodriguez, a citizen of Mexico; Anya Bauer, a citizen of Russia; Irina Lemetyuynen, a citizen of Russia; and Agnieska Koblenc, a citizen of Poland, have all provided interviews, and accepted responsibility for their actions, their part of the criminal scheme and have pleaded guilty to their respective charges as agreed upon as part of their plea agreements. Serguei and Irina, though they did not provide an interview, still accepted responsibility and were given a plea agreement and they too are ready to be sentenced according to the law. The investigation is almost over. Once we're done with sentencings and everyone serves what is doled out by the courts, if they have an immigration related charge, there will be detainers issued and they will then be turned over to ICE when their sentence is complete. If they are not sent to prison and don't have issues with ICE, then they go in their merry way and hopefully have learned from the closeness they came to spending a long time in prison. Now we wait and see what the courts decide.

On December 12, 2007, Irina Choukline, Irina Lemetyuynen, Agnieska Koblenc, all that pleaded guilty to the misdemeanor violation of Title 8, USC, Section 1306 (c), were sentenced in the United States District Court for the Western District of Missouri, Southern Division at Springfield, Missouri by Chief Judge Magistrate England. The sentencing for all three defendants were the same, six months' probation with credit for time served and no further supervision was necessary. John and I weren't totally satisfied with the sentencings, especially for Irina Choukline. We were under the impression that the other defendants were somewhat lured or manipulated into accepting so called leadership positions with the company and could understand their sentences. Irina Choukline however, Serguei's wife, played a much bigger role in the criminal scheme. She was the bookkeeper! All of the records were brought to her house for processing. She knew everything that her husband was doing, and still participated. Maybe the judge felt sorry for her because Serguei was traveling all over the world, had a wife in the Slovak Republic whom he had an apartment with and was providing money to. He had an immigration status in the Slovak Republic and now sounds like he had status in the country of Ukraine. If she and Serguei had gotten a divorce and decided to live together for the benefit of their son, she had to deal with him living in the same house and coming and going when he pleased to who knows where. Maybe the judge felt sorry for her and sentenced her to a lesser sentence so she could continue on without Serguei in her life. Only he knows the reasons for his decision.

Serguei Choukline, Anya Bauer, and Monica Lopez-Rodriguez, all of those who had pleaded guilty to felony charges will be sentenced later.

On February 22, 2008, Serguei D. Choukline was sentenced in the United States District Court for the Western District of Missouri in the Southern Division at Springfield, Missouri by District Court Judge Whipple to one count of a felony violation of Title 18, USC, Section 371, Conspiracy to Commit Title 18, USC, Section 1546, Visa Fraud. Choukline for this conviction was sentenced to twenty-seven months in federal prison with credit for the time he has already served while waiting for his sentencing date. Based on the plea agreement, and pursuant to Title 8, USC, Section 1228 (c)(5), Judge Whipple ordered Choukline upon completion of his sentence to be turned over to ICE, to be deported from the United States to Russia.

There were two possible plea agreements available to Serguei for this offense. If he had pleaded guilty to the number of visas he had actually applied for, over three hundred, he could have been sentenced up to ten years in federal prison. By pleading to the number of applications filed, eighteen, his sentencing guidelines was only around twenty-four to thirty-six months. Judge Whipple sentenced him to the mid-range of the guidelines. John and I would have rather seen him get the higher range especially for the way he treated his employees throughout these several years of misuse and maltreatment of them. One consolation was that as part of the plea agreement, Serguei accepted the stipulated Judicial Order of Deportation, which means that the Judge would order him deported back to Russia and there was no need to hold an Administrative Hearing for his deportation. Once he came to ICE custody, the Administrative Law Judge signed the Order of Deportation based on the District Court Judges order, and Serguei is deported back to Russia once arrangements are made.

On March 3, 2008, Monica Lopez-Rodriguez, was sentenced in the United States District Court for the Western District of Missouri, Southern Division, at Springfield, Missouri by District Court Judge Whipple for violation of Title 18, USC,

Section 1546, Visa Fraud. Lopez-Rodriguez, even though this was a felony offense, was sentenced to six months in federal prison and was given credit for time served. Since she had already served that time, she was not required to be sent to prison, or be turned over to ICE, as she had already been placed in removal proceedings, is out on bond, and was awaiting her hearing with ICE.

On May 29, 2008, Anya Bauer, was sentenced in the United States District Court for the Western District of Missouri in the Southern Division at Springfield, Missouri by District Court Judge Whipple for one count of a felony violation of Title 18, USC, Section 4, Misprision of a Felony. In other words, she knew that Serguei was committing Visa Fraud, and she failed to report it to law enforcement. For this conviction, she was sentenced to three months' probation. All of the defendants in this investigation have now pleaded guilty, been sentenced, and are heading off to do whatever for the rest of their lives. You would think we would be done at this point wouldn't you. Well, that is still not the case in this situation.

On June 20, 2008, since the appeal period has passed, authorization was requested and received from the courts to destroy remaining evidence associated with the investigation. On June 27, 2008, eight boxes of documentary evidence and one bag of computer media was destroyed. As far as the investigative stage of this investigation is completed and the case is now closed.

On February 3, 2009, Serguei Demitrivich Choukline, Inmate #18682-045, United States Federal Prison, Eden,

Texas, almost a year after his sentencing filed a letter with the Department of Homeland Security, Immigration and Customs Enforcement, relating to a case that he has against Michael Mukasey, who was at one time the United States Attorney General of the Department of Justice for an adjudication of his application for Naturalization in the United States. This claim, this was actually kind of funny, because at one time he told Irina Lemetyuynen, that he wasn't interested in obtaining citizenship in the United States because he has a status in the Slovak Republic and in Russia. He was only interested in the money in the United States to send it to Russia and the Slovak Republic. If I remember my Immigration Law correctly, as violation of Section 212(a)(6)(C)(i), Misrepresentation of a Material fact and seeks to procure or has procured a visa by fraud, which I think over three hundred obtained by fraud, would meet the elements of this offense, is deportable from the United States. His conviction of this offense and his acceptance of a judicial stipulated order by District Court Judge Whipple, renders him ineligible for becoming a Naturalized United States citizen. Anyway, Serguei in this request, is asking that all records associated with his application be released to him based on an Order to Show Cause issued by the District Court of Northern Texas.

On February 17, 2009, Serguei Choukline filed a motion to proceed without being required to pay fees, costs or give security because of his poverty, and his inability to pay the costs of the proceedings. He further stated that as a part of this motion that he receives no pay, no money, and no bank accounts.

On the same date, Serguei Choukline filed another motion with the court in the Northern District of Texas. In this particular motion, he referenced his conviction and sentencing on February 21, (actually on the 22nd), 2007, for a violation of Title 18, USC, 371, Conspiracy to commit Visa Fraud, in violation of Title 18, USC, Section 1546. As a part of this motion, he made several claims against the court.

He first claimed that he asked his counsel to appeal the sentencing guidelines, claiming that they had not been agreed upon by all parties in the plea agreement. Secondly, he claimed his counsel did not engage in adequate consultation with Serguei prior to sentencing. Thirdly, He claimed that his counsel did not dispute several important changes he wanted in his Pre-Sentence Investigation (PSI) Report during its preparation which he [Serguei] requested and he did not argue the disputes during the sentencing. Fourth, Serguei claimed that his counsel did not ask the court for downward departure from the sentencing hearing. As for the fifth allegation against his attorney that he filed with the court, he claimed that he is essential to the care taker of his 78-year-old mother. It is interesting that he claimed that he received not payment or expectation of payment for the smuggling, transporting, or harboring of any of the unlawful aliens, and claims he is eligible for the downward departure. It is interesting that he would make these claims against his attorney, because at sentencing, the United States District Court Judge, went to exhaustive lengths to ensure that Serguei had no complaints against his attorney and that he had received adequate counsel to which Serguei replied that he had no complaints. Lastly, he is requesting that he be moved, as he is being held in a higher-level security prison, because he is a deportable alien. A little side note, Serguei had also filed for an L1A, Intracompany Transferee Visa for his mother at a time she was in her 70's. It was denied and she too was placed in removal proceedings.

On February 19, 2009, The United States District Court for the Western District of Missouri issued an Order, in the case of Serguei Choukline, verses United States of America ordering Serguei to correct technical defects in the motion or face dismissal of this action. The order basically states that Serguei did not complete the request properly and that the request had to be filed on appropriate paperwork acceptable by the courts and directed him to make the appropriate filing by March 12, 2009.

Serguei filed a separate motion on the 20th to expedite the decision on his filing or he will have served his full sentence before a decision is made. On February 26, 2009, Serguei filed his motion on the appropriate forms with the District Court for the Western District of Missouri as requested. Based on this request, on March 6, 2009, the United States District Court for the Western District of Missouri filed and Order, directing the United States Attorney's Office to respond to the claims submitted by Serguei Choukline within thirty days of the order.

On March 11, 2009, AUSA David Barnes, the lead prosecutor in the investigation of Serguei Choukline in this case, entered his appearance as the attorney of record with the United States District Court. I don't know the date of the decision on these claims, but the court did not rule in favor of Serguei Choukline, and he served his entire sentence at the United States Federal Prison at Eden Texas.

Along with the motions and claims filed with the United States District Court for the Western District of Missouri at Kansas City, Serguei was also filing claims with the Department of Homeland Security, Immigration and Customs Enforcement. He requested that he be granted voluntary departure back to Russia instead of under an Order of Deportation. In other words, he requested that the Order or Deportation be removed, and he be allowed to return to his country without the execution of an Order of Deport. If that were allowed, Serguei would be able to apply to return to the United States again as soon as he wanted to. If he is deported, he is not allowed to apply to return for at least ten years.

On March 25, 2009, the Field Office Director for the Department of Homeland Security, Immigration and Customs Enforcement, Dallas Field Office, Dallas, Texas, responded to Serguei's Request, denying his request for voluntary departure to Russia, quoting that based on the plea agreement at sentencing to the Judicial Stipulated Order of Deport, and the issuance of that Order of Deport issued on February 28, 2008, he would be taken into custody when released from prison.

Serguei, I believe by this time has filed all of the motions that he can file. He is resigned to serving the rest of his sentence in the United State Federal Prison at Eden, Texas until his release from custody, at which time he will be turned over to the Immigration and Customs Enforcement, Detention and Removal Group to be deported from the United States.

The investigation is complete, so now it is cleanup time. Since Serguei was convicted of a Felony, and Irina, his wife, was convicted of a misdemeanor, it was decided to withdraw the request for the Asset Removal Group to cease any further consideration to seize the Choukline residence. Irina is taking care of not only their son, but the seventy-eight-year-old mother of Serguei.

Chapter Ten

Epilogue

The investigation of Serguei Choukline and all of his co-defendants is over, and the case is closed. What has happened to all of the players? What has happened to all of the foreign labor force that was misused and abused by the exploits of Serguei Choukline and MWHMC.

All of the foreign labor that has been identified throughout these two investigations, most have been arrested, administratively charged, and placed in removal proceedings to face deportation from the United States for overstaying their visas or for visa fraud. Many left on their own and returned to their home country. Those that have already returned to their country, may or may not have any remedy or benefit to apply for allowing them to remain in or return to the United States based on the way they were treated by Serguei as a victim of this type of control. They will probably have the opportunity to be considered for review. The manipulation that we are speaking of, is the keeping of their passports, putting them in a hotel room with several others, sometimes of the opposite sex, with just two beds and no privacy, expecting them to pay exorbitant amounts of rent to Serguei. They were then expected to pay him for their transportation to and from work, extra money to apply for their visas, which he did. He charged many other costs to the foreign laborer, and he lied in the applications by providing false and fictitious information for their extensions. He refused to pay them overtime. One time telling them that because they are temporary workers, they are not eligible for overtime, and then present them with a piece of paper to sign saying that they received their overtime pay, which went into the pocket of Serguei to fund his extensive travel overseas and to take care of his family, to heck with the welfare of his employees.

The abuse of Denis Butuzov, the humiliation of him in front of fifteen to thirty other employees, to intimidate them in case they expected to stand up to him as it relates to the way they are treated. Then when Denis, though he was afraid himself of Serguei attempted to recruit for me (which he was not forced to do), other foreign labor to come to me and be willing to testify in court or gather further information about Serguei and his business, he had a terrible accident. Yes, Denis was an alcoholic, and he knew it, and I believe that was part of his fear, that he would not be a good witness, but when he tried to tell others that Serguei was being looked at by an investigative agency, he mysteriously had an accident that put him in a coma. Not at any hospital, but at the hospital where Irina Choukline was an employee. If it had not been for Michael, my informant, who stepped in and spoke to the family and acted on behalf of the family as a translator, there is no telling what would have happened to Denis. Denis was subsequently flown back to Russia on a chartered plane because the hospital could not continue to take care of him, and his family wanted him home.

Employees of MWHMC had to, at times, wait weeks after they arrived in the United States to obtain work, and then when they did, were forced by Serguei to work seventy to eighty hours a week, if not at one place but at several with no overtime. Then when they complained, Serguei would continue with the threats that he was KGB, or Russian Organized crime. He would tell his employees that he had friends with the Police and with INS/HSI and if they continued to complain, he would have them arrested and deported from the United States. They would be sent back to their country. Which in fact, he had no authority to do. He as an employer could call INS/HSI and tell them he had an employee out of status who refused to depart for their country, but if that employee is arrested, there would be an interview process with that individual. If the interview is the type of interview I would expect to be done, Serguei would have signed his own opening of an investigation into his criminal activity.

As it relates to the claims by Serguei to his employees of being Russian Organized Crime leader/member, was it true? I have thought about that for years and I truly do not know the answer! There are Russian Organized Crime member who have been arrested and convicted in the United States in the past for visa fraud. One that stands out most is Vyacheslav Ivankov, who per open-source research, was actually a notorious Mafia boss, who had connections with Russian State intelligence organizations and their organized crime partners. He was subsequently arrested and convicted of extortion and visa fraud in the Brighton Beach area of New York City. He was deported back to Russian upon completion of his sentence and was in 2009 assassinated when leaving a restaurant in Moscow. A sniper rifle was found abandoned in a nearby parked vehicle.

Is this how Serguei saw himself, a Mafia member, KGB member, Organized Crime figure, or was it a figment of his imagination? Only Serguei and God, knows the truth to these claims. I can tell you I never saw Serguei without a shirt, so I don't know whether he had tattoos or not. Tattoos are common in the Russian Organized Crime arena of criminals and each tattoo has a significant meaning. If you look at any video of Ivankov, and see him without his shirt, there are a large number of tattoos exposed. Was Serguei truly ex-KGB as told to us by a Polish Consular Officer when he described his meeting with Serguei. A meeting related to several citizens of Poland that worked for Serguei and complained to the Polish consulate about their lack of wages. When this Polish consular officer met with Serguei in Springfield, Missouri for lunch, Serguei came out and told him that he was ex-KGB. Would an ex-KGB officer do that, I don't know, but maybe. Serguei claimed to his employees that he was a Russian Gang member and used his own admission that he had killed a person in Russia with his bare hands and had gotten away with it, using this claim to give the appearance that he was involved in the gang.

We were able, through my informant, to obtain a news article from the Premiere Newspaper in Vologda, Russia, the confirmation that Serguei did kill another person and the fact that he obtained a reduced charge and then amnesty for the conviction. The report being that Serguei paid $50,000.00 to the court to get this done was told to us by one of the persons that was interviewed. She told us information she had received from her own family in Russia regarding this claim. They had told her this happened and that is the same information we were hearing through our informant as well as information being spread through the Russian community in Branson and Springfield, Missouri. Did it happen? The ability to obtain truthful information from Russia, is a challenge, and still not known whether it is truthful or not.

Then there was the claim that Serguei was a Russian Naval Intelligence Officer on Submarines. This information was brought to our attention by a Source in the first investigation who himself was a retired high-ranking officer from the United States Army Intelligence Service. I certainly trust him when he tells me that he saw a photo in Serguei's residence of Serguei in a Russian Naval Intelligence military uniform standing with Boris Yeltsin, a future president of the Russian Federation. There were a lot of claims made by Serguei to get his employees to do as he instructed, to intimidate them with his background and experience. Was it all true? These are a lot of hats to fill or was it Serguei's narcissistic personality that he had to feel that he was this important to get the attention he felt he deserved and needed. I am not a doctor, and I don't profess to know the mind of Serguei Choukline, I only have what has been presented to me throughout these investigations as claims made to others directly from him, Serguei.

So, what has happened to everyone involved in this investigation?

Monica Lopez-Rodriguez, her mother, brother, and child, were all removed from the United States and returned to

Mexico. Monica, as a criminal alien after being convicted of a felony offense involving the fraudulent application for a visa, and her mother and brother for overstay of their B-2 Visitors visa. The child, though a United States citizen, being under the custody and care of the mother was sent to Mexico. When the child becomes an adult, he can return to the United States and claim his citizenship. The child can then file a legitimate application for Monica to return to the United States as the parent of a United States citizen, and it is the decision of the adjudicator as to whether or not, after all these years, would be approved.

Anya Bauer, a citizen of Russia, was also convicted of a felony, of knowing that Serguei was committing a criminal offense and failing to report it to law enforcement. This is a violation of immigration law, Section 237(a)(2)(A)(i), says if she is convicted of a crime involving moral turpitude within five years of her entry and is sentenced to a year or more, is subject to deportation from the United States. Though the sentencing guidelines did not allow her to be sentenced to a year, a felony is for a year and a day and therefore constitutes a deportable offense. That was the decision of the immigration lawyers, and she was placed in removal proceedings and was deported from the United States also as a criminal alien.

If a person is deported from the United State as a criminal alien, they can't even apply for permission to apply until after 10 years. They would then apply to the immigration office for permission and if granted, they can then apply for a visa to return to the United States. It is up to the adjudication officer reviewing the application to make that decision. This would apply to both Anya Bauer, and Monica Lopez-Rodriguez, if her child did not apply for her as the mother of a United States citizen.

As it relates to Agnieska Koblenc, she is a citizen of Poland and was convicted of making false statements on a visa application which in her case was filed as a misdemeanor. She too, because of a fraud in violation 212(a)(6)(C)(i) filing an application for a visa by fraud was placed in removal proceedings as well. Koblenc was allowed to remain in the United States and is living in Missouri.

As it relates to Irina Lemetyuynen, she is a citizen of Russia and was convicted of making false statements on a visa application which in her case was filed as a misdemeanor. She too, because of a fraud in violation 212(a)(6)(C)(i) filing an application for a visa by fraud was placed in removal proceedings as well. Lemetyuynen was allowed to remain in the United States and is living in Missouri. I believe both of these individuals were married to United States citizens and they were able to file on their behalf and they were granted status in the United States.

Then there is Serguei's wife, Irina Choukline. If Serguei had agreed to give us an interview and accept responsibility for his actions and the action of the company when he was first arrested, some of these misdemeanor allegations may not have been pursued as the primary target was Serguei Choukline and Monica Lopez-Rodriguez. They were the most involved in the criminal enterprise, bringing in and manipulating the foreign labor. But, as we continued with the investigation and conducted our interviews of Monica, Irina Lemetyuynen and Agnieska

Koblenc, we saw that Irina Choukline was just as involved as Serguei. She didn't do the traveling or the recruitment that Serguei did, but she conducted the bookkeeping. She is the one who made the deductions from the paychecks of all of the workers. They included deductions for transportation, rent, visa applications preparation, but there were no deduction's for taxes and proper insurance. She too knew the story behind Anton Kim because she was signing his name to paychecks along with Monica, Anya and Serguei. She is the person who disclosed the true identity of Anton Kim to Irina Lemetyuynen after Serguei and Monica's arrests. I am glad that we continued our pursuit of her, and I believe that she should have gone to jail along with her husband. On the other hand, was she forced to do these things under threats from Serguei? If Serguei was who he says he was, having the background he was purported to have, was she under threat to do the things that she was doing as it related to the business operation? After all, she was supposedly divorced from Serguei during the time that he was married to Martina Pirohova from the Slovak Republic, but Serguei was still allowed to live and reside in the same home. Again, she didn't give us an interview, but these are questions that we would have loved to ask her. She was charged, admitted her involvement, and was sentenced.

Irina Choukline is a Naturalized Citizen of the United States and a citizen of Russia by birth and was convicted of making false statements on a visa application which in her case was filed as a misdemeanor. She is not deportable from the United States or being charged with visa fraud or naturalization fraud. You may ask why not? Well, the answer is that because her visa was obtained long before this investigation began, we were unable to show any evidence that her visa was obtained by fraud or evidence to show that her United States citizenship was obtained by fraud. These benefits were obtained before she became involved in this visa fraud scheme with Serguei. Irina Choukline was allowed to remain in the United States and is living in Missouri.

As it related to the claims of her nursing certificate from Russia being a fraudulent document; the claim that she was nothing more than a dental assistant while in Russia; and the claim that she had only studied books for two or three years and tested to be a nurse in Alaska and had her license transferred to Missouri. As I said earlier, when I received this information, it was forwarded to the appropriate investigative agency as we would do with any crime that fell outside of our purview. It was forwarded to the State of Missouri Nursing Board for their investigators to look into. I was interviewed by the investigator about the documents that were forwarded to them and the claims that were brought to our attention during the investigation. The investigator was unable to verify the claims as it relates to the training that Irina received in Russia, although the stamps on her certificates and other documents appeared to be the same document stamps that Serguei had in his possession when we executed the search warrant on their residence. It was unable to be verified by the investigator. Irina did pass her nursing test in Alaska and was a nurse in good standing at the hospital where she was employed. The investigation was closed with no action taken and to the best of my knowledge, Irina is still a nurse in Missouri.

I now must discuss Serguei Choukline and his outcome. Serguei was his own worst enemy. His narcissism, or what appeared to be narcissism, his desire for recognition, his desire for control, power, and in his own words, the American dollar. The American dollar which he by his own comments is to send to the Slovak Republic and Russia. He had no desire to obtain citizenship in the United States.

In my research for this book, I found a news article dated May 3, 1995, from the Tulsa World, written by Mitch Maurer entitled "Russia Mafia Strength Detailed". In the first two paragraphs of this article, he states that he is speaking to a former Soviet Counterintelligence Official and identified Serguei Choukline as that person, who now lives in Joplin, Missouri and is trying to become a citizen of the United States but still stays in contact with his former colleagues. A little further down in the article, Serguei led the person writing this article to believe that he had entered the United States as part of an intelligence exchange program, which was nothing but a false statement, a lie! So Serguei himself either through truth or claim, purports himself to have an intelligence background as he spoke to in this presentation to the Tulsa Chapter of the American Society for Industrial Security as identified in this article.

We saw that Serguei had filed a motion with the then Attorney General Mukasey to make a decision in his application for naturalization in the United States. He did want to become a citizen of the United States, so he now says, but we never found any application information or proof of his application. Maybe it was his imagination! Again, based on his conviction, he was ineligible for it anyway. Serguei was convicted of a conspiracy to file 18 different visa applications for over 300 foreign workers and was sentenced to prison for this felony. As you can see from the last chapter, he filed several different motions claimed ineffective counsel in an attempt to have his sentencing reduced. It would not have changed the outcome. He was still only a resident alien in the United States and was subject to deportation based on his conviction.

Serguei accepted as a part of his plea agreement a Judicial Stipulated Order of Removal from the District Court Judge for the Western District of Missouri (In other words, there would be no immigration hearing. He has already been ordered deported), because of his plea to a felony visa fraud charge. He was ordered deported at the time of sentencing. Based on this order, a Judicial Order of Removal was issued on February 28, 2008, and the Warrant of Deportation was issued on January 27, 2009.

On November 24, 2009, roughly twenty-one months after he was sentenced, the Warrant of Deportation was executed and Serguei was picked up from Federal Prison in Eden, Texas, put on a flight with probably two deportation officers out of Dallas, Texas ICE Office and was escorted from Dallas to New York City. He would have been at that time, put on a flight by himself without any further escort, from New York City to Russia thus completing the execution of the order to deport of Serguei Choukline. However, I am sorry to report, that I received information through Michael, that Serguei had purportedly passed away sometime in 2014 by unknown causes. Serguei was a target of my investigation, and I was doing my job, but I never wish for the death of another individual under any circumstance outside of natural causes or war with an enemy. My heartfelt prayers go out to his family, and I pray that they are doing well after their loss. I would hope and pray that Serguei, before his death, saw the error of his ways and turned his life over to Christ and accepted Him as his Lord and Savior, but only God knows the answer to that.

As it relates to our informants during this investigation Michael and Darla, they were an asset to this investigation and were beneficial in finding Denis Butuzov, the employee that Serguei physically abused in a parking lot in front of as many as 15-30 of his employees for getting drunk and leaving a couple of other Russians stranded. We would not have known about him if it were not for Michael. We would not have had as much information of the visitors of Monica if it hadn't been for Michael and Darla and their periodic drives by her residence and providing this information to me especially after I returned to Kansas City, Missouri. Michael did have to appear at the United States Attorney's Office in Springfield, Missouri during the time we were preparing witnesses for court testimony. He was prepared to get on the stand and testify on behalf of the government.

Remember, when I met with them in the Restaurant, when he and Darla were having marital issues and needed someone to talk to. I later found that Darla had accepted Christ as her Savior at the age of 15 years old and was baptized on the same date. Michael had accepted Christ at the age of 6 years of age and was baptized later in life at the age of 25 years old. But this time when we had met, during a time that we all go through if you are married, they were able to rededicate their life to

Christ and save a marriage that was potentially headed down a path that would have been destructive. Instead of destruction, God allowed them to go through a reconstruction of their relationship and they have survived.

Michael and Darla still had their own immigration issues with which they were concerned about. They had applied for an immigration benefit that would allow them to remain in the United States, due to their fears of Serguei Choukline and any potential friends he may have in their home country. You may be asking what kind of problems they could have if they are from a different country then Serguei? Russia has an influence in many countries in the region of the world where they are from. Serguei, when deported back to Russia, could travel freely to and from these countries to include the country where Michael and Darla are from. Because of the assistance that they provided in this investigation; I took it upon myself to volunteer to testify on their behalf at their hearing before an immigration judge. I am very conservative, if you will, when it comes to someone from another country coming to the United States. If a person enters legally, uses their experiences to benefit this country and not become a detriment or have to live off of the government, that is great. They should be given the opportunity to apply and let the courts make the determination. It is a privilege not a right to be a part of this country and I knew from dealing with Michael and Darla, that Michael speaks four languages and Darla speaks five languages. I know, but I don't want to disclose how I know, that both of their families are involved in education and pushed it to their children because they wanted them, as most of us do as parents, to do better in life then we did. So, I testified in their behalf. I was able to tell the immigration judge that we would have had a more difficult time prosecuting Serguei than we did if it weren't for their assistance, as well as the other cases they helped me investigate. I told the judge that if Serguei were able to determine they assisted me in the investigation against him and if he did have all of the connections that he claimed to have, their lives, Michael, and Darla's, could be put in danger. After a few weeks of deliberation, the Immigration Judge ruled in their favor, and they were allowed to remain in the United States. They have subsequently become United States citizens and are doing very well and have proven themselves to be an attribute to the United States of America. Michael has a degree in Philosophy and is involved in several different business ventures and Darla has a master's degree in finances. They have done very well in their careers and have been an asset to the United States.

They now have two children. I have been retired for almost 10 years and since that time, Michael and Darla have become good friends to my wife and me. As a matter of fact, their oldest son was given my name for his middle name. It is an honor when one of your own children gives a grandchild part of your name. That is your heritage, which is your own family and a blessing that will always be uplifted to God and thanked for. Especially watching your own grow up and make something of themselves. When someone other than family respects you enough for the way you treated them with respect and they decide to give one of their children a part of your name, it is a different kind of honor. I, at the beginning, when I first met them, believed they could benefit my investigation and help me get to the point where I would get a prosecution of Serguei.

But I treated them with respect! I listened to what they had to tell me. I listened when they were having marital problems and tried to help them through scripture finding their way back to the biblical principles of marriage and what God has in store for them. Many would say, 'Ah, you just did all of this because you wanted something from them.' That is not the case. I like to think that I am serious about my work. This is not the kind of person I am. It was truly heartfelt when they were having marital issues and I wanted to help. I showed them a respect as I would hopefully show anyone else, and they appreciated that kind of attitude and showed me respect in return. They gave me the honor of having one of their children named after me.

Michael and Darla are a special kind of people and would put many Americans to shame because of their work ethics alone. I saw them at times working three and four jobs while going to school to survive and were still providing me information in the investigation of Serguei and others. My wife and I, two years ago, were given the privilege of being the Godparents to Michael and Darla's two children and watched them be baptized after having accepted Christ as their Savior. We live in different states, but we have the opportunity to text back and forth between me, Michael and his son and share scripture and discuss God's word. Their son graduated high school a year earlier than he should have, and due to his extra classes graduated not only with a high school diploma but the equivalent of a two-year degree and is now in college seeking a four-year degree. He is also attending a six-month training period in his church, studying to be a deacon. I could not have testified on behalf of a better couple to obtain a benefit in the United States and become citizens of this great nation. They are truly in love with the United States and appreciate every benefit they have been able to obtain but, it is mostly attributed to the time invested in hard work. Not because of me, but because of their love of the Lord, and the United States and the effort they themselves have put forth.

Michael did tell me recently that he has spoken to the brother of Denis Butuzov, the person that Serguei assaulted in front of his other employees. He was told that Denis is still alive but, is still in the coma that he was put in because of the car accident. The Russian community blamed this accident on Serguei Choukline. Did he do it? Was he behind the accident? I don't know but, it is believed by the Russian community in Springfield and Branson, Missouri that he was.

Gale Gaines, and Joyce Harris, of the Missouri Department of Labor, Division of Employment Security, continued their employment with the State of Missouri as far as I know, we all lost touch after the completion of the investigation. Gale Gaines and Joyce Harris who assisted Gale in this investigation were each given a Certificate of Appreciation from the Department of Homeland Security for their assistance in this investigation. John and I had asked their assistance in this case not to be disclosed until after everyone was indicted. So, on April 25, 2008, in the internal news for the Missouri Career Center, it was revealed that Gale and Joyce were given the Certificates of Appreciation for their assistance in providing information that led to the 17-count indictment against Serguei Choukline and others on the visa related fraud charges.

As far as the co-case agent in this investigation, John Cress, with the United States Department of Labor, I could not have asked for a better person to work with through this investigation. Though he and I have lost touch since I retired 10 years ago, last I heard, he was still working at the Department of Labor, chasing people like Serguei, and working any type of case involving fraud against the legitimate worker of the United States. He had been a good friend as we worked side by side throughout the entire investigation. We together, voiced our complaints or concerns to the United States Attorneys in this investigation. Some arguments we won and some we didn't. The fact is, that we were in full support of each other throughout the entire case. If I followed up on a lead, he was always notified and informed of the outcome and vis versa if it was the other way around. When we were getting ready to execute the search warrants on Monica's residence and then Serguei's later that evening, we were both fully committed to get our agencies on board with the number of persons needed for the safety of all involved. We didn't finish and get back to our hotel until around 1:00 AM. There were never any complaints about long hours or the number of trips that had to be made from Kansas City, Missouri to Springfield, Missouri. Even those surprise trips that were only a couple of days apart. John was a good friend and a great co-case agent and if I were still working and had another case with the Department of Labor, I would be asking if he was available.

Our United States Attorneys were superb when it came to prosecuting Serguei and pursuing search warrants, subpoenas, trial subpoenas, witness prep as well as interviews and plea agreements. I know I was kind of hard on Bruce Clark in the first investigation of Serguei, and I didn't totally agree with his decision to shut down the first investigation, but I did support his decision. He would have been the one who prosecuted the case. He was the one who would have had to put on the evidence before a jury, to convince them that Serguei was indeed a criminal and warranted prosecution and conviction. I was always taught from the days of the academy with INS and all the training I had received from the Department of Homeland Security and to my days of training with the United States Air Force, Office of Special Investigations (AFOSI), once the United States Attorney's Office accept the investigation, they are in control. If they determine there is not enough to pursue the case and get to prosecution, then there is not enough there. That was the case with Bruce Clark, and I respect his decision in that aspect of our pursuit of Serguei Choukline.

As it relates to our second investigation of Serguei, Bruce and David (who I will speak of next), worked well together as United States Attorney's. They were in continued discussions with each other, at least what I saw and when I would speak to them about a particular matter, they would say things like "Let me bounce that off so and so." Though David was the person I spoke to most of the time, if one of them wasn't available, I could usually reach the other. When it came to getting our trial subpoenas, (the subpoenas that are issued to a witness to come to testify in trial), we were all, that is Bruce, David, me, and John, there together discussing each witness and their interviews, the testimony they would be able to provide to determine if a subpoena were to be issued or not. Then once the subpoenas were issued and John and I served each of them, which was about 40, the witnesses were called in for trial prep, everyone was there together, working closely with each other in coming to the best decision available for the case. Thanks to Bruce for his hard work and dedication and the closeness that we were able to develop throughout this investigation, Serguei Choukline was convicted, sentenced, served his time, and was deported from the United States.

David Barnes, whom I have stayed connected with over the years, was the main attorney in this investigation and the primary point of contact for all requests such as, filing affidavits for search warrants, requests for subpoenas, charging information, indictments etc. He was the go-to guy. I know he was involved in a lot of different things associated with the United States Attorney's office, I know he and I both enjoyed talking about firearms, shooting at the range, speaking about the military, and a lot of similar likes. So, we had a lot of discussions during the lunches that we were able to take, as well as all of the trips to Springfield, Missouri and back from attending hearings and preparation for trial. He is the first that I have seen, but I am sure there are others, who have responded with agents to search warrant executions. He was adamant, that he could not enter the residence, but stood by on the outside for any legal questions that may come about. He was a staunch advocate when he argued for the reconsideration of Serguei's detention status after finding that he was married in the Slovak Republic and that he had other identities and businesses in different names. When it came to prosecuting the case in Springfield, instead of Kansas City, Missouri, he argued that it should be prosecuted in Kansas

City as that is where the Strike Force Office was located and would be beneficial to the proceedings.

The United States Magistrate, who had just been temporarily promoted to Chief Magistrate Judge for the Western District of Missouri, ruled that it would remain under his jurisdiction in Springfield. We also found that the defense attorney for Serguei was supposedly a classmate of the magistrate. Is that the reason it was retained in Springfield? I don't believe so, but it sure caused a lot of extra travel and trips to Springfield for the agents and prosecutors. It could be the decision was made because the judge knew of the hardship the trips to Kansas City would put on those defendants that had little or no money. Whatever the case, David was an advocate for justice in the case and was an attorney to be reconciled with in court.

I spoke with my superiors at Homeland Security and asked that we provide plaques and letters of appreciation to both David and Bruce, as well as John, which was approved. I went to John's office with my Assistant Special Agent in Charge (ASAC), we thanked John for his hard work in this investigation and gave him a letter of Appreciation and a plaque as well. The same was done for David Barnes and Bruce Clark, the prosecutors of Serguei and those who assisted in this investigation. The ASAC and I traveled to the United States Attorney's Office in Kansas City, Missouri and met with the Supervisory AUSA. It so happened that most of the United States Attorneys were in some sort of training that day, and the Supervisory AUSA wanted the presentations made in this class in front of the other attorneys. They, David, and Bruce, deserved the recognition for their hard work in this case. This is not a flashy case for many attorneys, it's not drugs or mobsters or terrorists etc., but it is a crime and like most financial investigations it takes a lot of time to work. It is basically a paper case. A lot of reading and comparing one paper, one application to another and comparing the lies to the truth that has been given to us or determined through other means. It is not appealing to a jury in many instances, but, Paul Becker, their supervisor, wanted this recognition in front of the other attorneys.

The ASAC gave me the description of the case to read to the other attorneys and the individual letters of appreciation to read to them as well. Then he, the ASAC, presented the plaques and letters to them. They or course received a big round of applause. Probably from some thinking, glad it was them and not me, and from others a heartfelt congratulations, and from some, hopefully a "Hmm, maybe I ought to think harder about these types of cases." I don't know the answer to that comment, but I hope that this caused attorneys to look harder at accepting immigration related cases or cases from the Department of Homeland Security that now deals with these investigations. I truly enjoyed working with all of these attorneys and agents from these different agencies to bring a conclusion to this case. I hope that anyone else that works a joint investigation of this sort are truly blessed with the cooperation that was, I hope, had by all in this case.

As for me, what have I done? Well, I completed this investigation, but prior to its conclusion, after I returned to the Kansas City Office, was asked to switch from immigration related investigations to those of a National Security nature.

Looking into illegal exports and imports of arms and technology. People like Chinese that steal information from their jobs off of computers and send back to their country to be used against the United States. I did not know this, but there is a crime intitled Deemed Export. What is a deemed export? A deemed export is the release of restricted or regulated information to a foreign national. Even though that person is physically in the United States at the time of receiving the information.

While an export is generally considered to be materials, information and technology that leave the country, something can be a deemed export without leaving the country. If regulated information or technology is released to a foreign national living in the U.S., it is deemed to be an export to the home country or countries of the foreign national.

This concept holds true for industrial espionage situations as well as national security concerns. The Export Administration Regulations (EAR) state that, an export of technology or source code (except encryption source code) is 'deemed' to take place when it is released to a foreign national within the United States. Technology is 'released' for export when: it is available to foreign nationals for visual inspection (such as reading technical specifications, plans, blueprints, etc.); when technology is exchanged orally; or when technology is made available by practice or application under the guidance of persons with knowledge of the technology. This is considered a violation of Section 734.2(b)(2) of Export Regulations.

Other offense that may be investigated as part of this assignment are violations of the International Traffic in Arms

Regulations (ITAR), which would be investigations related to weapons technology, and or the actual weapons being exported without proper authorization, as well as any product being exported outside of the United States without proper export license or attempting to export to a country that has Presidential Order denying export to a particular country due to their support of terrorism or a terrorist organization.

Remember, I was one of those who thought the move to combine INS and Customs into the Department of Homeland Security was a good idea, so I was excited to be asked to move to the National Security Group to be involved in these types of investigations. Unfortunately, for the writing of this book, many of the types of investigations that we were involved in, or informants used are classified and cannot be discussed, but you get the idea anyway. I did get to investigate an unclassified export violation, and who knows, maybe the subject of another book down the road.

I took a transfer to Washington, D.C. in 2010. I finally made it! Something that I always wanted to do was to get to headquarters, to be a part of the decision making and hopefully help to make needed changes or so I thought. I accepted a position in the Office of International Affairs, Visa Security Program as a Program Manager. It was a promotion for me, and since I was close to retirement, I thought it would be a good move. Go to DC, get my last three years at the promotion grade, retire, and move back to my home state of Missouri and start a new part of my life. I took the promotion, went to some training that I probably should not discuss, and was sent to Saudi Arabia on a thirty-day detail to work in a program reviewing visa applications of persons wanting to travel to the United States. Attempt to determine if they are eligible to travel to the United States or not. Do they have some other baggage in their life that would stop them from coming and refer those individuals to the State Department there on site for their review. I was sent to Jeddah, on the Red Sea. That was pretty cool, because as a Christian, you know about the Red Sea. The Red Sea is the sea that was parted by Moses in the Old Testament during the Exodus of the Israelites from Egypt to the Promised Land. Though this was a long way from my location, just the fact that I am this close was exciting to me as I could look out of my hotel window and see the sea, though I was a little worried too.

I was put up in a hotel in downtown, probably a 15-minute drive from the Consulate where I was assigned. The consulate was attacked in 2004 by terrorist and had been closed until this year and was now being reopened. I was, I think, the second temporary officer to be on this detail waiting for the officer that was actually going to be assigned fulltime to this position. I was met at the airport in Riyad by the guy that was my supervisor, and he transported me to the hotel several miles away in Jeddah. As we entered the hotel, there was a security guard who wanted to check our vehicle, but since it was a United States Government Vehicle, he had no authority to search it. Across from him was an Armored Personnel Carrier, with a machine gun mounted on top. Sometimes it was visually manned and other times it was not. I was picked up every morning by an armored car and transported to and from the Consulate. This caused me a little concern, I was actually glad that my detail was only for thirty days.

At the end of my thirty days, I returned to DC to fulfill my duties there. I was not a match for DC. I rented a house in Fairfax, VA. My home back in Missouri was on the market. It was about this time that the housing market fell and houses in Missouri were not selling. I had a couple of offers on my house, but they were ridiculous offers, not anywhere near the value of the home even with the crash. My house sat empty for the year that I was in DC. Our daughter checked on it regularly, making sure the water ran and there were no leaks. Our grandson mowed for me every week or so, but the house just wasn't selling. We were paying all the house payments, utilities, insurance, and any maintenance that needed to be done on our home in Missouri. In Virginia, we were paying our rent, rental insurance, and utilities there. I will tell you the cost of living in Virginia is substantially more than in Missouri to the tune of about double.

After about eleven months, there was a job announcement that came out stating that if we wanted to put in for a job outside of DC and pay our own move and take a demotion, to submit this application. Of course, I spoke to my wife, and she agreed. I was leaving my home in Virginia at about 7:00 AM, drive 10 minutes to the Metro Stop, take an hour-long train ride to whichever metro stop is close to the office I was working in that day, and then usually walk about four or five blocks to the office. At the end of the day, I would walk the four or five blocks to the metro station, an hour-long ride home and then the 10-minute drive home. I was expected to work ten hours a day, so with the hour train ride each way, ten hours working almost 30 minutes in a vehicle, I was gone almost thirteen hours a day. I know it was my choice to put in for the job and take the offer when it came. I was close to retirement, and I needed to think about the end of my career and our stability.

As part of the application process to go back to the field, I had to list the three places I wanted to go and of course I chose the primary as Kansas City where my home was still empty. I was subsequently selected to go back to Kansas City, Missouri and eventually left Washington DC. Since it was after my first year, I was able to maintain pay parity and was able to be paid a lower grade, but close to the pay I was being paid in DC, of course minus the cost of living from DC to Kansas City, Missouri. I returned to my old home, was put back in my same National Security Group and even had some of my old cases returned to me. I was back home. It was 2011 and everything seemed to go back in time a little bit, as I returned to my old church, everything as if I hadn't even left. There were other cases over the next year and a half that I worked, and in December of 2012, I ended my career in the federal government and retired with 35 years in law enforcement. It was a heartfelt departure from the government. I enjoyed my work and wished at the time that it wasn't over, but I was close to mandatory retirement and wanted to go on my terms and not have an eviction notice hung on my office door by someone who was waiting to take over my office space. Everyone that I worked with over the years were a pretty good bunch of agents and officers. Like any law enforcement family, we had our disagreements and a few arguments here and there, but overall, it was an exciting opportunity for someone who only had an associate degree and wanted to do nothing in life but be in law enforcement. This was just not the path I thought I would be taking. My wife is much more at ease these days, as I am not being called out at all hours of the night or working 24 to 48 hours straight, not waiting for phone calls to find out where I am or when I am coming home. Raising our three children, may as well say, by herself between my career as an agent and along with my Military career until I retired in 1999. I owe a great deal to her for her support and as I said at the beginning of this book, will never be able to repay her or my children for all they had to deal with during my career.

SOURCES

The Joplin Globe, February 23, 1993, Russian Company Opens Joplin Office, Joplin Globe Staff

The Joplin Globe, March 14, 1993, Russians Are Coming Here, Harlan Snow

Tulsa World, May 3, 1995, Russia Mafia Strength Detailed, Mitch Maurer

The Joplin Globe, November 28, 1997, Russian Police Plan to Visit Area, Robert J. Smith

The Joplin Globe, December 7, 1997, From Russia with Love, Robert J. Smith

The Sedalia Democrat, February 11, 2004, Two Charged Over Fraudulent Visas, Springfield AP

The Premiere, March 10, 2004, American Werewolf, Unknown Author

The Slovak Spectator, July 4, 2005, Businessman's Best Friend – Chamber of Commerce – Chamber of Commerce are an Essential Part of Doing Business, Marta Durianova

Springfield News Leader, February 9, 2006, 2 Accused of Illegal Worker Scheme, News Leader Staff

Springfield News Leader, February 10, 2006, Indictment Claims 300 Immigrants Falsely Received Documents, Katheryn Buckstaff and Nina Rao

Branson Agent, June 29, 2007, Polish and Russian Immigrants Arrested for Branson Smuggling Ring (2005 Archives)

Open Source

United States Citizenship and Immigration Services, History Office and Library, Overview of INS History, 2012

History Channel.com, December 21, 2018, U. S. Immigration Timeline, History Channel Editors

Immigration and Ethnic History Society, Immigration History, 2019

www.ingramcontent.com/pod-product-compliance
Lightning Source LLC
LaVergne TN
LVHW011815060526
838200LV00053B/3793